Destiny Road

DESTINY ROAD

The Gila Trail and the
Opening of the Southwest

ODIE B. FAULK

OXFORD UNIVERSITY PRESS
New York   1973

Map Design By David Lindroth

Copyright © 1973 by Oxford University Press, Inc.
Library of Congress Catalogue Card Number: 73-82666
Printed in the United States of America

For RICHARD
a Southwesterner, and
For LAURA AND NANCY
who have traveled the road often

Preface

Today television brings us a summary of the day's events, while newspapers and magazines help to place the world picture into sharper focus. In this era of instant communication and of daily mail deliveries, it is almost impossible to understand how the arrival of a stagecoach could be as important as it was in California in the 1850s. But to the men laboring there at that time—two to three thousand miles removed from their families and from major sources of news—the arrival of a stage was a major event. It brought passengers from whom one might learn about happenings in the vast outside world, and it brought mail.

"God, a letter from home!" wrote one enthusiastic pilgrim laboring in the California mines in 1857. "I cried for happiness just to hold it in my hand. I could not bring myself to open it until the next day." Said another, "Even bad news from home was better than no news at all." A third echoed the thirst they had for American and world news: "What's happening out there? We want to know, and we have the right to expect the government to provide the means for this."

The road over which this mail came prior to the Civil War was the same one over which the successful Forty-Niners planned to return to their homes in the East or over which their loved ones would travel to California to join them. This was the Gila Trail, and to these men it indeed was a destiny road. Many of them had traveled it to reach California; it was this same route which stagecoaches crossed to bring them mail and a way home; and it was the Gila Trail which promised the best and most practical route for a transcontinental railroad; and that would link California permanently with the rest of the Union. That the Gila Trail should be of such importance was incomprehensible to men in the eastern United States during the 1850s, for there rivers had provided the natural highways for pioneering; these in turn had carried canoes, flatboats, keelboats, and steamboats, and along their banks men had planted their farms and built their cities. In the arid reaches of the American Southwest, however, no such water route was available, and a road, such as the Gila Trail, became the route of exploration, conquest, transportation, and communication.

And in the process of crossing this arid land that is southern New Mexico, Arizona, and California, some of the travelers, freighters, stage line workers, Civil War soldiers, telegraphers, and railroad hands began to alter their thoughts about the region. What once had seemed a fit home only for Indians and a few hardy Mexican frontiersmen began to seem a suitable home for more and yet more Americans, some of whom even realized the peculiar beauty of the region. Thus the opening of the Gila Trail as a means of rapid transportation and communication to the mines in California in turn brought about the settlement of a vast territory by tens of thousands of miners, farmers, ranchers, and businessmen; no longer would it be home only to a few hundred residents huddling in the few small towns. Thereby the Southwest became a productive part of the United States. Mighty cities would grow where earlier there had been only way-stations for the Butterfield Overland Mail, and cattle would graze on hills and valleys that earlier had supported only a few wild animals. The history of the American Southwest in large measure is a story of transportation, communication, and settlement along this one road—indeed a trail of destiny for the region.

In the writing of this book I had extraordinary help and cooperation from the Library at Oklahoma State University; without this aid I would never have been able to complete the work. Also, I thank Don Bufkin of Tucson, Arizona, from whose maps I generously borrowed in compiling those in this book, while the Arizona Historical Society in that same town generously made available many of the pictures contained herein. And I acknowledge

viii

with gratitude the deft editorial staff of Oxford University Press, particularly that of Sheldon Meyer, who has done much to improve this work.

Finally, this book is dedicated to my son Richard, who took a special interest in it as it progressed through the various drafts, and to my wife Laura and my daughter Nancy, with whom on many occasions I have traveled the highways that parallel the Gila Trail. My wife, as always, proved indispensable through her encouragement and patience—and her willingness to read the manuscript first to catch my mistakes of spelling and typing.

Stillwater, Oklahoma.   O.B.F.
Spring 1973

Contents

Destiny Road

1

A Road of Great Value

Lieutenant Colonel Philip St. George Cooke was worried on the morning of December 16, 1846, and with good reason. True, the Mexican garrison at Tucson, Arizona, which he was approaching, had only 200 soldiers, and he had some 400 men at his command. Yet the young American officer did not believe his troops were loyal to the United States or to him, and he knew that they were not adequately trained to do battle. In fact, he so distrusted his men that in the two previous months he had refused to allow them to carry loaded weapons despite the fact that they were crossing enemy territory. But he did intend to go through Tucson, even to purchase food there, so he issued orders for his troops to load their rifles, and the march toward the town began.

A slim, erect soldier of six feet, four inches, Cooke surveyed the land around him. What he saw added to his feeling of unreality about the battle to come, for the geography was very different from the parts of the United States that he had seen. Giant cacti strained toward the sky, some of them with one or more branches "gracefully curved and then vertical, like the branches of a candelabrum," as he described them. Spanish daggers and other weird plants grew out of sand that seemed never to have tasted rain, and the trees had bark as green as their leaves. In the distance the mountains, their tops capped with wintery snow, appeared like giant pieces of paper, crumpled and scattered with little order; some ran north and south, others east and west. Creek beds and arroyos lined their sides with wrinkles, but in December they carried no water. Only the nearby Santa Cruz River was flowing, but it was little more than a small stream; it appeared as if by magic, flowing from the distant mountains of Mexico, but even this was strange to the Americans, for it ran from south to north.

All thoughts of this strange geography left Cooke's head as two Mexicans were sighted coming toward the Americans. The question now was whether or not a battle would soon be fought. The night before Mexican soldiers had come from Tucson with word that their commanding officer, Captain José Antonio Comaduran, would oppose the Americans if they tried to come through the town. But, said Comaduran, if Cooke and his troops would march quietly around Tucson, he would not try to stop them. Cooke had replied that the Mexicans should deliver up a few arms "as tokens of a surrender" along with a promise that they would not "serve against the United States during the present war."[1] Cooke's intent was to purchase food in the city, for the men of his command were in need of food.

Tension doubtless mounted among the Americans as they waited to hear what word the two Mexicans were bringing. Would it be an armistice, or would it be battle and fighting and dying? To the great joy of the men, the two messengers announced that Captain Comaduran and his soldiers had abandoned the city and its fort, forcing most of the civilians to go with them; they had even taken the town's two brass cannons with them. Thus Tucson was open to the Americans without a fight.

As Cooke and his troops entered the outskirts of the little village, the only settlement for 300 miles to the north, east, and west, a growing number of Mexican civilians gathered around to escort the newcomers to the center of town. Cooke paused near the first cluster of houses to tell the local citizens, through an interpreter, that he had not come to make war on them, that he would show justice and kindness to unarmed civilians, and that individual property would be respected. After this speech, soldiers and Tucsonans went through the dusty streets to the central plaza; there Cooke ordered the public stores of food opened to his men, some of whom proceeded to eat themselves sick on boiled wheat and the other items—"Flour, Meal, Tobacco, Quinces"—which the townspeople brought to the American camp as a gesture of goodwill.[2]

4

Philip St. George Cooke late in life.
From Twitchell, Leading Facts of New Mexican History (1912).

Cooke decided to remain in Tucson for two days to allow his men some needed rest. During that first day Cooke apparently toured the area, for he wrote a description of the town and the valley. The Tucson he saw was not impressive. The fort, an old Spanish *presidio,* was built in the form of a square, enclosed by ten- to twelve-foot-high walls some 750 feet long. These walls were three feet thick at the base, constructed of adobe bricks, measuring four-by-twelve-by-eighteen inches, held together by mortar of a dark brown color. The soldiers' quarters were along the south wall, the roof serving as a parapet as did the roofs along the other three sides. Stables ran along the north wall, while civilian homes were adjacent to the east and west walls. Only one gate allowed entry; above it was a station for a sentinel. Other buildings were scattered inside the city, including the church, which measured some ten by twenty feet. Three plazas gave open space for drilling the troops, dancing, courtship, and other recreational activities: the *Plaza Militar* in front of the stables, the *Plaza de las Armas* before the soldiers' quarters, and the *Plaza Iglesia* before the church. Only one store was inside this enclosure, a saloon dispensing mescal owned by Juan Burruel. Outside the walls of the fort were three other stores, which sold items that were perhaps less necessary, along with houses that were little more than huts; these were lined along narrow streets that wandered off toward the small farms in the valley. Wheat was grown in the vicinity, along with corn, pomegranates, and quinces.

Few of the huts inside the city had windows. Doors generally were made of brush or cactus ribs tied together with rawhide. A small fireplace in a corner of each house served as cookstove and source of heat. The residents generally slept on the floor while wrapped in blankets. Chairs and tables were in short supply, as were most types of furniture; therefore meals were served on the floor or on the ground outside the hut. Perhaps a trunk or chest held the family's scant possessions, which seldom included more than a few pieces of clothing, cooking utensils, and religious objects. Cock fights, horse racing, observance of the local patron saint's day, gambling, and *fandangos* (dances) provided relief from the tedium, hard work, and danger which constituted the lives of the residents of Tucson.[3]

The major worry in Tucson at this time, as it had been for the years since its founding in 1776, were the menacing Apaches nearby. Cooke tried to capitalize on this fear by promoting a little sedition while he was in the vicinity; that day of December 17 he paused to write a letter to be delivered to Captain Comaduran upon that worthy's return. "Be assured that I did not come as an enemy of the *people* whom you represent," wrote Cooke. "The unity of Sonora with the States of the north, now her neighbors, is necessary effectually to subdue these Parthian Apaches." In short, he was suggesting that Sonora's interests lay more with the United States than with Mexico.[4]

That same evening of December 17 the men's rest was disturbed by a report that "a large Mexican army was coming." Cooke hastily ordered "assembly" blown and tried to calm his officer in charge that night, who had grown so excited that he had shouted, "Beat the drum, beat the drum—if you can't beat that drum, beat that fife." Cooke restored order and sent a company into town to reconnoiter. When no one returned to report, he sent a second company to find the first. All eventually returned to report that no armed Mexicans were in the area. The only casualty that night was loss of sleep.

The next day, December 18, Cooke and the Americans departed northward, marching down the Santa Cruz River toward the Gila. Their passage through Tucson and their two-day stay there in mid-December of 1846 was not significant in itself; they had not raised the American flag, nor did they leave men behind to occupy the region permanently. Seven years would pass before, by treaty, the area south of the Gila River came under American jurisdiction. Thus Cooke and his battalion were only transients passing through on their way from New Mexico to California. Yet this two-day stay did signal the end of one era of Southwestern history and the start of another. For more than three centuries the region had been

7

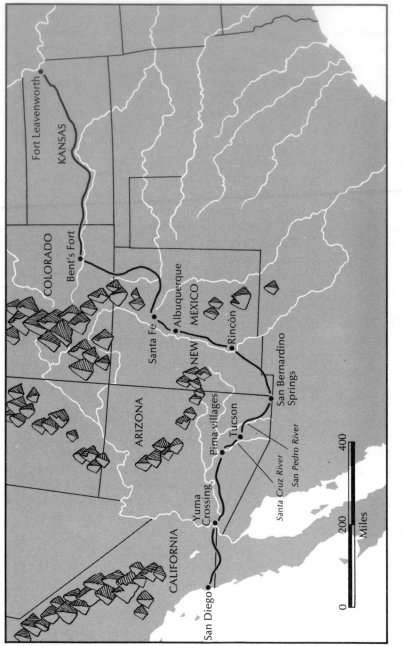

1. Route of the Army of the West from Fort Leavenworth to Albuquerque, and Cooke's Wagon Road from Albuquerque to San Diego.

Spanish and Mexican, while for eons previously it had been the sole property of various Indian tribes, principally the Apaches. Thereafter it would be American territory.

Prior to the arrival of the Apaches, there had been other Indians living in southern New Mexico and Arizona, but their identity is lost behind the mists of time and the total absence of written records. Anthropologists generally believe that the Apaches migrated from northwestern Canada sometime between A.D. 900 and 1200; members of the Athapascan linguistic group, they still have cousins in western Canada, Alaska, and along the coast of Washington and Oregon, while yet more of their cousins would continue a southward migration to become the Aztecs of Mexico. Once in their desert homeland that is now the American Southwest, the Apaches scattered from western Texas across southern New Mexico into southeastern and east-central Arizona. Gradually after their arrival they split into a number of sub-tribes, or bands, each with a slightly different dialect, but all with a similar lifestyle.

To the east were the Lipan Apaches and their allies, the Kiowa Apaches, who roamed western Texas northward to Kansas. In northern New Mexico were the Jicarilla Apaches, while the Mescalero and Warm Springs Apaches controlled the southern part of that area. The Chiricahua Apaches lived in southeastern Arizona and considered themselves virtually the same tribe as the Warm Springs group. And, finally, there were the western Apaches of central and east-central Arizona: the White Mountain Apaches, the Cibecue group, the Coyotero Apaches, and the San Carlos Apaches (themselves subdivided into the Pinal, Arivaipa, and San Carlos bands).

When these Apaches came into the Southwest, they lived by hunting and gathering, eating small game and wild plants. The eastern members of the tribe soon learned to supplement their diet with buffalo meat, and they adopted many of the living habits of Plains Indians, such as the tepee and the horse culture. The western Apaches continued to live in brush shelters, known as wickiups, borrowed the practice of weaving baskets and making pottery from the Pueblo tribes, and even did some farming; but they never really

9

became "horse" Indians. Instead they developed great endurance at traveling on foot and living off the sparse products of the desert. Everywhere, however, there was one feature that distinguished the Apaches: their ferocity in battle and their habit of supplementing their economy by raiding other tribes. Endlessly they warred on the Pueblo Indians of New Mexico as well as natives (and later the Spaniards) to the south and the desert tribes of Arizona: the Pima, Papago, and Maricopa groups. Their name itself, Apache, came from a Zuñi Indian word meaning "enemy," although they referred to themselves as *"Diné,"* meaning "the People."

For these tribes and sub-tribes time passed quietly after they entered the Southwest. They fought with each other and with Nature for a hard existence. Yet their lives were not altogether bleak and brutish. For them there was the pleasure of the hunt and what to them seemed the beauties of geography: mountains and valleys, lakes and deserts, towering pines and stunted cacti—a harsh land of incredible wonder for him who looked. Their lives were uncertain when game grew scarce, crops failed, or battles went against them. They suffered from disease, from occasional famine, and from man's cruelty to man. Such was all the life they had ever known, however, and they found reason within it for hope, for laughter, for dreams.[5]

The years of sole Indian ownership of the Southwest ended in the late 1520s because of a Spanish failure to find gold in Florida. In November 1528 some eighty survivors of an expedition to Florida, trying to reach Mexico by means of crude, self-made barges, were cast ashore on the coast of Texas, probably at Galveston Island. More dead than alive, their bodies aching from thirst, hunger, and exposure, these men were at the mercy of their accidental hosts, the Karankawa Indians, begging for shelter and food. Only fifteen Spaniards survived that first winter, and they were forced into slavery as a reward. Six years passed before one of them, Alvar Núñez Cabeza de Vaca, could mature plans for escape.

In company with three other survivors, Cabeza de Vaca set out walking from the vicinity of Galveston Island. After eighteen weary months of walking, first to the northwest, then due west, and finally to the southwest, the four were rescued at a frontier outpost in west-central Mexico by slave-catching Spaniards. Taken to Mexico City, Cabeza de Vaca reported to the viceroy that he had not seen any evidence of great wealth in the region he had traversed, but that he had heard rumors of seven golden cities somewhere to the north. Thus was born the entrancing tale of the Seven Cities of Cíbola which would lure so many Spaniards northward during the next century.

The viceroy sent a small expedition to check on the rumors that Cabeza de Vaca had heard. Fray Marcos de Niza, a Spanish Franciscan missionary, entered Arizona from the south, accompanied by friendly Indian allies. His report to the viceroy in September 1539 was sufficiently optimistic to trigger the famous expedition of the following year, the one commanded by Francisco Vásquez de Coronado, who likewise would cross much of the Southwest without finding any gold or silver. His pursuit of the Seven Cities of Cíbola, as well as yet another fabled land of wealth, the Gran Quivira, took him across Arizona, New Mexico, the Texas Panhandle, Oklahoma, and into central Kansas. The failure of the Coronado expedition meant that once again the land would be controlled solely by its native inhabitants. Yet the enduring and enticing legend of fabulously wealthy cities somewhere to the north, places where even the rudest peasants ate from golden plates and where the streets were paved with silver, would linger and periodically would bring conquistadors and their sons and grandsons back through the region.

The Spanish settlement of Mexico gradually moved farther and farther north from Mexico City during the decades following Coronado's trek, finally pushing a finger of colonization northward into New Mexico in 1598. That year Juan de Oñate brought four hundred soldiers, civilians, and Indian allies to found a town in the vicinity of Santa Fe (which itself would be established in 1609). Oñate in his explorations also would reach into Kansas as well as southwestward to the Gulf of California at the mouth of the Colorado River; with the same curious motivation that drives tourists yet today, Oñate would pause at El Moro (Inscription) Rock to carve his name there and the message *"Paso por aqui"* ("I passed here").

This first settlement in what is now the United States was fol-

11

lowed in 1690 by the colonization of Texas, in 1693 in Arizona, and in 1769 in California. Most such expansions of the Spanish empire were made not because of any need for additional land to farm or to gather more Indians as citizens for their king nor yet even to convert these natives to Christianity; rather such colonization principally was accomplished because of fear of foreign settlement. The Spaniards wanted to keep the French out of Texas and the Russians out of California.

The blood of conquistadors ran in the veins of these pioneer settlers of what the Spaniards called the *Provincias Internas* (Interior Provinces). They were brave men and women who faced all the dangers that American frontiersmen of a later age would face, and they did so with a civilization little advanced over that of their Indian adversaries. Yet the Indians still retained real ownership of the region, for the Spaniards never were able to link this region with an east-west road. And there were men of vision in the 1770s and 1780s who saw the need for such a route of transportation and communication, just as there were men of courage who would attempt the task.

Coming to Arizona in 1768 to assume charge of Mission San Xavier del Bac (at Tucson) was Father Francisco Garcés, a Franciscan missionary. Not quite thirty years of age, Garcés in 1772, while on a trip of exploration westward, crossed the Colorado River and pushed to the vicinity of the present El Centro, California; there, to the west, he could see two gaps in the Sierra, and there he met Indians who told him of white men to the west. These, Garcés knew, were his countrymen who had settled California just three years earlier. He concluded that there was an easy overland route to California, and in company with Captain Juan Bautista de Anza, presidial commander at Tubac, Arizona, he petitioned the viceroy for permission to pursue this project. The viceroy gladly approved the request, for he knew that such a road would be of great benefit to the future of California, which was linked to Mexico only by tenuous and difficult sea routes.

On January 8, 1774, Captain Anza, Father Garcés, and thirty-four soldiers set out from Tubac. With the aid of the Yuma

Juan Bautista de Anza, the Spanish soldier who explored
so much of the Gila Trail and who colonized San Francisco.
Courtesy Arizona Historical Society.

Indians they crossed the Colorado River, and arrived at Mission San Gabriel (near Los Angeles) in the spring. Returning to Arizona, they were commissioned to take settlers and supplies to California over the new road. This they did in late 1775 and early 1776; the settlers they took founded the city of San Francisco. Father Garcés did not complete that second journey, however; instead, he chose to remain among the Yuma Indians and work to convert them to Christianity. Working there early in 1776, Garcés conceived the idea of linking Santa Fe and California by an overland route, and on February 14 he set out to make it a reality. Up the Colorado he walked for fifteen days, then turned west across the Mojave Desert to reach Los Angeles late in March; then, with no European companion, he returned to the Colorado, crossed it, and made his way across northern Arizona to the Hopi Indian pueblo of Oraibe. Confronted with Indian hostility which prevented his going further, he paused there on July 3, 1776, to write a letter to his Franciscan brothers in New Mexico saying what he had done and suggesting that they try to open a road from New Mexico to California. Garcés then returned to the Colorado, went down it, and returned to Tucson. In eleven months he had covered 2000 miles.

Father Francisco Silvestre Vélez de Escalante, the Franciscan missionary at the Zuñi pueblos who received this letter, thought the idea a good one and requested permission from the governor of New Mexico and his ecclesiastical superior to follow it up. Permission was granted, and the expedition, which consisted of Father Escalante, a fellow Franciscan named Francisco Atanasio Domínguez, and a militia captain, Bernardo Miera y Pacheco, with six soldiers, departed from Santa Fe on July 29, 1776. The party turned into southwestern Colorado to avoid the troublesome Navajos and entered what is now Utah; in December, they found themselves at the Great Salt Lake with few supplies left, and Indians in the area knew nothing of the Spaniards to the west. Thus they returned to Santa Fe, their expedition a failure; no northern road would be opened to California during the years of Spanish rule.

At this time, the Anza-Garcés road to California by way of

14

Yuma Crossing was in use. But because its continued existence depended on the goodwill of the Yuma Indians, the Spanish officials who controlled the destiny of this region in 1780 authorized the establishment of a colony at the junction of the Gila and Colorado rivers. Within a year, however, quarrels had developed between the Yumas and the Spaniards, and the resulting discontent came to a head in July 1781. On the seventeenth of that month the Yumas clubbed soldiers, priests, and civilians to death and destroyed the small Spanish settlement.[6] Thus ended the usefulness of Anza-Garcés overland route to California, and California was left to develop along far different lines than other Spanish areas of the northern frontier. Having as its only way to Mexico a sea that was difficult to cross, California was left to its own resources and its own devices with no strong loyalties ever developing between it and the rest of Mexico. A good east-west road over which more settlers and soldiers, along with Spanish officials, might have moved would have made that province an integral part of the Spanish empire and probably would have changed the subsequent history of the American West.

Without this east-west road, New Mexico's only link with any other Spanish province was south to Chihuahua City and Mexico City. The governor of New Mexico found that it took three to four months to send a hard-riding messenger to Mexico City and receive an answer, while teamsters needed eighteen months to make a round-trip from Santa Fe to Mexico City in their huge, ungainly carts. Similarly in Arizona, the route of transportation and communication was southward to Arizpe, Sonora, and down the western slope of the Sierra Madre Occidental through Sinaloa to Guadalajara and Mexico City. Little wonder then that the Indians were the real owners of most of Arizona, New Mexico, and California. Neither missionary nor soldier was able to subdue the native inhabitants during the seventeenth and eighteenth centuries; both cross and sword failed to conquer the lordly Apaches.

However, the Spaniards in their centuries of ownership did leave a strong imprint on what would come to be the American Southwest. They introduced horses, cattle, and sheep, and they es-

15

tablished the ranching industry. They blended their architecture with that of the Indian to produce the unique styles which still give the Southwest a strong regional flavor. Their foods became a mingling of Indian and Spanish—corn and chiles, along with beef—while the names they gave to rivers and mountains and towns are still heard. The soft strains of the guitar yet dominate southwestern music, and the ancient tongue of Castille and León, of Granada and Andalusia, is still spoken. Spain did not own the land entirely (although it and other European nations thought so), for the Indians were the real masters of the Southwest. In reality the area was an ethnic melting pot. The Indians changed most but the Spanish social and cultural heritage also was in a state of flux.

This Spanish heritage did not end abruptly in 1821 when Mexico won its independence from Spain and with it ownership of the American Southwest. In fact, to the Indians there doubtless seemed no real change at all. The same Spanish-speaking people still lived on a small part of the land; their religion remained Catholic, their architecture was the same, their customs and food and dress and music and way of life were unchanged. Even the government and the soldiers continued to operate in exactly the same fashion. But there were subtle changes. Under the Mexican constitution of 1824, New Mexico became a territory, its governor appointed in Mexico City just as previously he had been appointed in Madrid. Then in 1836 the region was designated a "department," which meant about the same measure of self-government as before: very little. Thus New Mexico would continue until 1846 and the arrival of the Americans. The two major cities in New Mexico were Santa Fe and Albuquerque, neither of which had attained great prominence. Santa Fe was but a typical Spanish village with a large Catholic cathedral dominating all. Albuquerque was but slightly larger and of no better appearance.

Technically, there was no Arizona during the Mexican years just as there had been none prior to 1821. Under the constitution of 1824 there was one Mexican state in the Northwest called El Estado Libre de Occidente (The Free State of the West), which included the present Mexican states of Sonora and Sinaloa along

16

with what is now Arizona. By 1831, however, the Sonorans had become so unhappy that their state (and Arizona) was separated from Sinaloa and given separate statehood. This political fight was of little interest to the people around Tucson, however, for theirs was a struggle for daily survival. The officer who commanded the presidio not only was the military commander for the region but also served as the chief civil and judicial official; in reality, he functioned as a lieutenant governor for the region.

Only in California was there any sign of prosperity during the Mexican years. This came more from neglect than from design. The state, as it was designated by the constitution of 1824, was still isolated, and politicians in Mexico City were too concerned with their own fights for power to worry about controlling California. Left to itself, with few Indians to fight, the Californians grew rich selling the hides and tallow from their cattle, which ran wild and which increased in numbers without work on the thousand hills of the Sierra, to American and British shippers.

Even in this period, however, there were attempts to link New Mexico to California by an east-west road, just as there was one effort to open a route through Arizona to the West Coast. In the years 1823-26 Captain José Romero, commander of the presidio at Tucson, and Father Felix Caballero, a Dominican serving at Mission Santa Catalina in northern Baja California, attempted to reopen the Anza-Garcés road. Because the Yuma Indians were yet hostile, Romero and Caballero crossed the Colorado near its mouth, but there also they found the natives untrustworthy. They reached California safely, only to be prevented from making their return to Arizona for three years by Indian uprisings in inland California and by tribal warfare among the Indian nations along the Colorado River. Although Romero was promoted to lieutenant colonel for his effort and was widely hailed as a "Mexican Anza," the trail he used remained closed except for the briefest of intervals.[7]

Ironically the one road to have any use in all these years was the one Father Garcés had failed to open: one from Santa Fe across to Los Angeles. This was opened by Antonio Armijo of New

17

Mexico as a result of the Santa Fe trade. Missouri traders came annually to New Mexico with goods, and one item they were willing to exchange these for was the mule. In the early years following the opening of this trade in 1821, the supply of mules in New Mexico had seemed inexhaustible, but before the end of the decade the demand had far outstripped the supply. Thus in 1829, in an attempt to secure still more mules, Armijo organized a party of sixty men and a large pack train of New Mexican goods, mostly blankets and *serapes*, which he took overland to California. In the process he opened a route from near Santa Fe northwestward to what is now the Four-Corners Country (where Colorado, New Mexico, Arizona, and Utah come together today), then went west along the present Arizona-Utah border to the Virgin River, proceeded along the northern bank of the Grand Canyon, passed by what is now Las Vegas, and crossed the Mojave Desert to Los Angeles. New Mexicans soon were crossing this route regularly, but their goal was strictly economic; they wanted mules, not social or political ties with the West Coast. And always, these contacts were at the unofficial level.

By 1846, therefore, the Mexican provinces of New Mexico and California, along with Arizona (which was part of Sonora), were isolated and thinly populated. The population of California was a mere 5000, Arizona had only about 600, and New Mexico could count about 30,000. The roads were little improved since the days of Spanish control, and there were no reliable maps of the region.

Then came the entry of Americans in 1846, the result of a war between the United States and Mexico which began that year. The causes of this conflict were far removed from the Southwest; rather they can be traced to a clash of cultures, to the claims question (the debts owed by Mexico to American citizens which Mexican officials refused to pay), to the question of the boundary of Texas, and to the unwillingness of Mexican politicians to seek a peaceful solution to the issues separating the two nations. In fact, some Mexican politicians were deliberately seeking a war, for thereby they hoped to gain power at home—and because they be-

18

lieved they could win a war with their neighbor to the north. French military advisers had told these Mexicans that they could win such a war, for Mexico had four times as many soldiers in its army as did the United States, soldiers who were better trained and who were armed with more modern weapons. Thus these Mexican politicians were saying that they would see "the Eagle and Serpent" (meaning the Mexican flag) flying over the White House before they would negotiate a settlement. President James K. Polk of the United States tried every honorable means to secure a peaceful resolution to the quarrel, but in this he was unsuccessful. Only when he learned that Mexican troops had crossed the Rio Grande to attack American soldiers did he go before Congress to ask for a declaration of war. This was voted on May 12, 1846—some three weeks after the secret Mexican declaration of hostilities on April 23.[8]

Once the war with Mexico began, President Polk quickly moved to take New Mexico and California—especially California, which he had been trying for a year to acquire by diplomacy. To head this military expedition, he authorized Colonel, later General, Stephen Watts Kearny to organize the "Army of the West." This Kearny did at Independence, Missouri. With this army of slightly less than 2000 men, he marched to Santa Fe where Governor Manuel Armijo surrendered without a shot being fired. This accomplished, Kearny divided his army into four parts: the first to remain at Santa Fe as an army of occupation; the second under Colonel Alexander W. Doniphan, consisting of Missouri Mounted Volunteers, to march south to Chihuahua City and then east to link up with the troops of General Zachary Taylor; the third, consisting of 300 dragoons, Kearny would lead personally to California to conquer it; and the fourth, to be under the direction of Lieutenant Colonel Philip St. George Cooke, was the Mormon Battalion, and its task was to open a wagon road from New Mexico to California.[9]

At first glance Cooke's orders seemed to have little to do with winning the war with Mexico or even with the conquest of California, but General Kearny apparently recognized that California would never be securely American until it was linked with the rest

19

of the Union by a usable road, one over which not only horses but also wagons could travel. Otherwise, the only way goods and the mail could reach the West Coast from the East would be by sea. And in 1846, almost seven decades before the opening of the Panama Canal, this was a voyage of 18,000 miles which took some six to eight months to accomplish. A road for transportation and communication thus was absolutely necessary, and thus Kearny's orders to Lieutenant Colonel Cooke.

In fact, Kearny so recognized the vital importance of this road that he chose one of his best officers to command the effort. Cooke in 1846 was thirty-seven years of age. Born in Leesburgh, Virginia, on June 13, 1809, he had graduated from the United States Military Academy at West Point at the age of eighteen (class of 1827), and then had seen service in various Indian wars in the Midwest and in Texas and Arkansas. Moreover, he had even been into New Mexico prior to 1846, for three years previously he had been assigned to protect the Missourians bound for Santa Fe from raiding Texans (who claimed New Mexico east of the Rio Grande and who wanted to collect the customs duties on this traffic); for this effort Cooke had received a personal message of thanks from the president of Mexico, Antonio López de Santa Anna. And in 1845 Cooke had accompanied Colonel Kearny on a trip of exploration to the Rocky Mountains; on this they had traveled 2200 miles in ninety-nine days. Thus In 1846 Cooke was an experienced and able officer, one who knew frontier conditions from first-hand experience and one who could command the respect of the men serving under him.

For these reasons, especially the latter, Kearny named Cooke to command the expedition that would open a wagon road from Santa Fe to San Diego, California. A strong commander was necessary, for the troops to be used to accomplish this task were the five hundred men who made up the Mormon Battalion. These were the men from the Church of Jesus Christ of Latter Day Saints, commonly called Mormons, who had enlisted in the army in order to help their church at a time of crisis. This sect had been organized in New York in 1830 by its founder Joseph Smith. Gradually they

20

had moved westward to escape persecution, first to Ohio, then to Missouri, and finally to Illinois. There at their city of Nauvoo they had prospered—until 1844 when Smith was murdered. Then, under the leadership of Brigham Young, their new prophet, they had started in 1846 the move that would take them to their new home in Utah; eventually they would transform this desert and make it bloom. Yet money to finance this move to Utah was so desperately short that Young had written President Polk to offer the services of five hundred of his followers for the army; their term of enlistment was to be twelve months, and their pay was to go directly to their church (to help finance the move to Utah).

When these Mormons joined the American army, however, they had little reason to love the United States. Non-Mormon Americans had persecuted them, had murdered Joseph Smith, and had taken the Mormons' homes at Nauvoo. Cooke realized, when he assumed command of the battalion, that his men were of doubtful loyalty—just as he noted, when he first inspected them, that they were undisciplined, tired, and poorly clothed, and that their mules were in a sad state. Eighty-six Mormons he found totally unfit for the march to California, and these men he ordered left behind in New Mexico. Therefore, when he departed Santa Fe on October 21, 1846, it was with slightly more than four hundred men. His destination, San Diego, was some 1100 miles away across an unknown desert wilderness without known road or trail. In his wagon train he had only sixty days' rations of flour, salt, sugar, and coffee; salt pork for only thirty days; and soap for just twenty days. He did have a large quantity of rope, tools, shovels, and picks, however, for he intended to get his wagons through to California even if the Mormons had to dig a road much of the way in order to accomplish it.

That morning of October 21 he ordered the bugle blown early so that the wagons could begin rolling by 8:00 a.m., but an hour was lost in rounding up nineteen cattle and fourteen mules which had strayed. The same problem would occur on many mornings on the trail. And in the next few days, as they marched south down the Rio Grande covering about ten miles a day, several mules

21

broke down to the point of no longer being serviceable. Moreover, rain and wind delayed the column, and the men grew sullen. Probably there would have been a mutiny against Cooke had not Brigham Young solemnly enjoined his followers to remain obedient to their army officers.

On that first several days' trek down the Rio Grande, Cooke learned much both about his men and his equipment, yet the question uppermost in his mind was neither the grumbling Mormons nor his dwindling supplies; rather it was when to swing his column to the west. This was no idle decision to be made lightly, for even his guide, Antoine Leroux, could not tell him where the geography was both suitable for wagon traffic *and* had water available. Leroux was a former mountain man who had been across the region by horseback, and he knew where water could be found; but often the water was in places inaccessible to wagons, while the flat desert country that would allow vehicular traffic had no water on it.

Finally on the morning of November 10, more by instinct than by reason, Cooke gave the order to swing away from the river and head southwest. Very quickly the task of finding additional water became the paramount concern for the entire column. Leroux and his scouts went ahead searching, and their directions forced the battalion more toward the south; in fact, they soon were heading more toward Janos in the Mexican province of Chihuahua than toward San Diego. Finally Colonel Cooke grew impatient that he was not heading more directly toward California, and he roared, "This is not my course. I was ordered to California and I will go there or die in the attempt!" Turning to his bugler, he ordered, "Blow the right." The column thereupon turned more directly westward.

On this new course they found water some days, but on others they did not. When the evening camp was dry both man and beast suffered. At Playas Lake (in present Hidalgo County, New Mexico) all did get to drink their fill. Then, soon afterward, the American column came upon an old Spanish road, little more than a cart trail; it had been used to drive cattle from San Bernardino Ranch (almost exactly at the spot where Mexico, Arizona, and New Mexico join) to Janos, Chihuahua. The column followed this trail and arrived at an abandoned ranch early in December. There the soldiers found cattle gone wild on the 65,000 acres that had been granted in 1822 to Ignacio Perez; the attempt at ranching had failed owing to Apache hostility. Some of the animals were shot to provide badly needed beef for the men's diet.

Although some of these animals provided food, others provided excitement—almost too much of it. A few of the tough old bulls decided to attack the Americans. One private was tossed into the air and received a dangerous wound in his leg. The same bull gored a mule before it was felled by rifle fire. And one enormous bull charged at Cooke. A corporal shot it, and it died almost at the commander's feet. Other casualties in this encounter included a sergeant who received some broken ribs, and Lieutenant George Stoneman (later to be governor of California) who in his excitement almost shot off his thumb with his rifle. Cooke in his journal dryly referred to the encounter as the battle of "Bull Run."[10]

There also Cooke encountered Manuelita and a few Apache braves. Their Spanish was barely understandable (Cooke commented that it was communicated in a "brutal grunt"); the Indians agreed to trade but only for blankets. Soon the Mormons were doing a brisk business trading their blankets for *tiswin,* a native beer of fair potency. Cooke tried to halt this traffic but was not totally successful.[11] Moreover, when the battalion departed San Bernardino on the afternoon of December 4, the men were so angry at not being allowed to finish curing some meat that they wandered away from the column to shoot at wild cattle; there even was some hint of mutiny. Cooke responded by ordering all muskets unloaded.[12]

Gradually the column then moved on westward, some of the Mormons loading their weapons despite their commander's orders. They sweated and heaved the wagons through the mountains and high deserts until they came to the valley of the San Pedro River. There on the morning of December 12 the guide Antoine Leroux returned with information he had received from a group of Mexicans he had found making mescal (an alcoholic beverage manufactured from cactus juice). They had told Leroux that at Tucson there was a Mexican army fort with two hundred soldiers in it; normally such a Mexican fort had only fifty soldiers, but the news of an American approach had caused an additional 150 troops to be sent north to aid in repelling them.

Two days later, on December 14, this information was confirmed when a small party of Mexican soldiers arrived from Tucson. They said they had been sent by their commanding officer, Captain José Antonio Comaduran, to tell the Americans that they could not come through Tucson; however, said Captain Comaduran, the transients would not be molested if they would march quietly around the little town. Cooke replied to the messengers that Comaduran's terms were unacceptable, for his men needed supplies. When the messengers departed, Cooke ordered the troops issued twenty-eight rounds of ammunition apiece, and they were given brief instructions in loading their weapons and in deployment tactics. Moreover, he felt it necessary to remind his men that they had not come to make war on unarmed Sonorans; they would overcome any resistance, he noted, but "the property of individuals you will hold sacred."[13]

That evening of December 14, two officers came out from Tucson, one of them Captain Comaduran's son. They came, so they told Cooke, to arrange an armistice. Cooke responded that the Mexicans should surrender and the town be opened to his men for trade and refreshment. To this the Mexican officers replied that Cooke's terms were unacceptable, after which they departed. Thus the Americans approached Tucson on the morning of December 16 expecting to fight only to be greeted by civilians with news that Comaduran and his troops had abandoned the city. After two days' rest, Cooke and the Mormons departed northward down the Santa Cruz River toward the Gila. On December 21 they arrived at this stream to find the Pima Indians in the area both friendly and willing to sell supplies to the Americans.

From the junction of the Santa Cruz with the Gila it was 118 miles to Yuma Crossing. There they found the Colorado River almost a mile wide, which made for a very difficult crossing. For

San Diego in the 1850s. *Courtesy Library of Congress.*

Tucson, Arizona, as seen by John Bartlett in 1852.
From John Bartlett, Personal Narrative, II.

this purpose the Americans used a pontoon boat to ferry the men across, while their supplies were carried on crude rafts which the men fashioned from trees growing along the river bank. In connection with these rafts Cooke was given an opportunity, rare on this trek, to show his sense of humor. One raft with Mormons on it began drifting dangerously downstream. The colonel, watching from the shore, shouted instructions to the men aboard: "Try the other side," he yelled when he saw that the Mormons could not reach the river bottom with their poles. They did as he said, but they could not reach the bottom on that side either. Cooke thereupon took off his hat and waved at them, shouting, "Goodbye, gentlemen! When you get down to the Gulf of California, give my respects to the folks!" And off he rode without a backward glance.[14]

Finally, however, wagons and men all were across the broad river safely, although several mules were drowned in the crossing. This feat was accomplished in the dead of winter with an inch of ice on the river where the current was not too swift. Yet the major geographical obstacles were still ahead, desert and mountains which would make the river crossing seem tame by comparison. Immediately to the west of Yuma Crossing were the sands of southeastern California, a strip some fifty miles wide that matched the Sahara Desert of Africa in its dunes of shifting and blowing sand. Cooke feared his command, man and beast alike, would die for want of water on this incredible stretch of sand, but the troops continued to dig deeply at points where they found a few trees growing, and always a trickle of the precious liquid was found.

It was on this hard desert crossing, moreover, that Cooke and his men heard of the battles which General Kearny had fought in California.[15] Rumors thereupon began to circulate through Cooke's command that the battalion would arrive at its destination only to be captured by Mexicans and made prisoners of war or else be killed. Such talk naturally made the men grumble the louder at the hard work they were being forced to do to get the wagons across the sand. Once past this section, the Mormons entered the Imperial Valley, itself a desert but welcome in comparison to the sand dunes

26

just behind. They found some water in this region, and with it came a revival of hope. Then on January 18 they had very welcome news; from San Diego came word that Americans were securely in control there and that food and supplies were awaiting the Mormons.

Before they could arrive on the Pacific Coast, however, there was one last range of mountains to be crossed, the coastal Sierra. This last obstacle would almost accomplish what the desert to the east had failed to do: to stop the wagons. At the first pass, as the battalion ascended the range, Cooke found his way blocked; the path he was following was too narrow for his wagons. He was determined to go forward, however, and ordered men with picks and shovels to widen the pass. The Mormons sweated and strained, but the walls were of rock and defied their efforts. Cooke thereupon ordered his men to take the wagons apart and carry the pieces through to be reassembled on the far side. Beyond this first pass were others equally narrow, but with the help of picks and shovels—and even ropes, which were used to lower the wagons down sharp cliffs—the battalion moved westward. They fought cold weather in those mountains, the rain threatening to turn to snow at any moment. Tents were blown down during the nights by hard winds, and weary Mormons were cheated out of their sleep. Mules died, and others strayed. But onward they went, encouraged by the thought of food awaiting them at San Diego.

At last on January 29, 1847, Cooke brought his exhausted men into that town, their wagons still rolling. There he had the bugler blow assembly, and to the men he read the report he had prepared for General Kearny about their march of 2000 miles: "History can be searched in vain for an equal march of infantry," he said. "Half of it has been through a wilderness where nothing but savages and wild beasts are found, or deserts where, for want of water, there is no living creature." And, he concluded, not only had he and his men made this crossing, but also they had dug wells along the way, wells which would be of great help to future travelers. But their major accomplishment was the wagon road which they had opened from Santa Fe to San Diego. ". . . Marching half naked and half fed, and living upon wild animals, we have discovered and made a road of great value to our country."[16]

In this process of opening a wagon road, Cooke and his Mormon troops had come to understand and to appreciate one another much better, even to the point of having respect for one another. The American commander was lavish in praising the men who during the course of the journey had threatened to mutiny against him. And the praise was richly deserved, for those Mormons had undergone the most severe physical hardships and had survived it to accomplish their mission. Moreover, the Mormons, for their part, had learned that Cooke was nòt altogether the rigid disciplinarian and stiff soldier, but a warm-hearted man who was concerned about their welfare. (Today in Salt Lake City, there is but one statue of a non-Mormon: that of Philip St. George Cooke.)

Philip St. George Cooke was correct in reporting to General Kearny that he and his men had opened a road "of great value to our country." In fact, this would prove to be an understatement. The Virginia soldier could not have known that just one year later gold would be discovered in California and that the wagon road which he and the Mormons had pioneered, one that would come to be known as Cooke's Wagon Road, would be one of the major overland routes to the new West. But Cooke did realize the vital importance of a route of transportation and communication across the desert Southwest, something absolutely necessary if California ever was to become a productive part of the United States; this he knew without foreknowledge of the discovery of gold. In 1848 California was considered valuable because it had harbors from which American ships could engage in the Oriental trade; if this trade was to prosper, the Pacific Coast needed some form of transportation with the East. Cooke had provided that.

As Cooke had traveled across the Southwest, he had seen little practical value in the land between Santa Fe and San Diego. The desert to him was an unfortunate impediment to be traversed as rapidly as possible. Little could he know that this stretch of desert would itself become valuable in the future. Technology eventually would enable men to farm the desert, just as ranching would flourish in the same region eventually. Thanks to the mineral riches of the land, as well as to the potential for farming and ranching, that desert interval between New Mexico and California would some day be filled with people, and Cooke's Wagon Road would be the artery of settlement—just as it surprisingly would contribute to the final boundary settlement between the United States and Mexico within just seven years.

2

The Road Becomes American

A glance at a map of the present United States shows that the boundary between this country and Mexico takes peculiar turns and twists for no known geographical, social or economic reason. Colorful stories have been told to explain such meaningless jags as that just west of Nogales, Arizona, where the boundary turns to the northwest to run in a straight line to the Colorado River just south of Yuma. One version has it that the surveyors working on the boundary were drunk on tequila and thought they were still going due west, while another says that these men were hot and thirsty and simply decided to survey in a direct line to Yuma, the nearest place where they could get cold beer. However, it was not drunkenness or the desire for beer that explains the final course of the boundary; rather in large measure it was the location of Cooke's Wagon Road that figures prominently in the setting of this dividing line.

When the two countries ended their war in 1848, their representatives signed the Treaty of Guadalupe Hidalgo to bring hostilities to an end. In this agreement, concluded on February 2 that year, a new boundary was drawn. This was to begin three marine leagues out in the Gulf of Mexico, proceed up the deepest channel of the Rio Grande to the southern boundary of New Mexico, run due west for three degrees of longitude(approximately 178 miles), turn directly north to the nearest branch of the Gila River, and proceed down the deepest channel to that river's junction with the Colorado; from that junction the boundary was to run in a straight line to a point one marine league (3.5 miles) south of the harbor of San Diego. That same treaty provided that each nation was to appoint a commissioner and a surveyor whose task it would be to

Major William H. Emory of the Corps of Topographical Engineers.
Courtesy Arizona Historical Society.

John B. Weller, who served as the first American boundary commissioner.
Courtesy Arizona Historical Society.

run and mark this new boundary. And the record of their acts, when all four had signed, would "have the same force" as the treaty itself.[1]

Early in 1849, before he went out of office on March 4, President James K. Polk decided to appoint the American surveyor and commissioner, else the positions would be given to Whigs by the incoming administration of Zachary Taylor. Polk's first choice for the position of boundary commissioner was Major William H. Emory, a member of the army's Corps of Topographical Engineers. Pictures of Emory taken during the Civil War show a portly gentleman with a large mustache, piercing eyes, and stern face; yet in 1849 he was one of the most experienced and able men in the United States in the fields of surveying and mapmaking. Also, he was familiar with the American Southwest, for he had served in Kearny's Army of the West that had marched to California in 1846. A native of Maryland, Emory, a West Pointer, was thirty-eight years old when Polk made the offer to name him boundary commissioner, but to accept the post meant that he had to resign his commission in the army. He refused. Nevertheless, Polk wanted him to serve on the boundary commission and thus named him the chief astronomer and cartographer on it.

Polk's second choice for the post of boundary commissioner was Ambrose H. Sevier, United States senator from Ohio who had been defeated for re-election in November 1848; but Sevier died before his appointment could be confirmed by the Senate. Polk thereupon named John B. Weller to the position. Weller had just been defeated in the race for the governorship of Ohio, his home state, and needed some kind of job. During the recent war with Mexico, Weller had shown considerable competence by rising from the rank of private to that of colonel strictly on his ability; he was a man of merit and one accustomed to command, but he equally was a political appointee—and the president's third choice for this delicate task.

Polk's choice for the job of surveyor was better, and the man he chose first did accept the offer: Andrew B. Gray. Born in Norfolk, Virginia, in 1820, Gray had helped survey the Mississippi

Delta while still a teenager, after which at age nineteen he had emigrated to the Republic of Texas. There he continued his education and became an eminently qualified civil engineer and surveyor. In fact, at the age of twenty he was selected the surveyor representing Texas on the commission running and marking the boundary between that republic and the United States. Then, leaving the Lone Star Republic, he had worked on the survey of the Keweenaw Peninsula of Michigan, after which he returned to Texas to become a member of the famed Rangers who were fighting the Indians.

Also going with this United States Boundary Commission was young Amiel Weeks Whipple, another member of the Corps of Topographical Engineers. A graduate of West Point, class of 1841, and a soldier, he was to assist Emory in determining the latitude and longitude of every position on the maps that were drawn of the boundary. Whipple never was able to forget his upbringing in Rhode Island, however, for during the trek across the Southwest he carried an umbrella to protect himself from the rays of the sun— and even wore white gloves while doing his field work. Lieutenant Cave J. Couts, an infantry officer who commanded the soldiers sent to protect the surveyors, commented, "Poor Whipple! Times are hard on him. Ambulance, Umbrella. Oh, My!"[2]

These men, along with their assistants and the soldiers, set out for San Diego, California, where they were to meet with their Mexican counterparts. Their journey supposedly was to have been a quick one: by boat to Panama, then overland, and finally by ship to California, but they found this passage very difficult because by the spring of 1849 there were thousands of gold-hungry Forty-Niners also trying to get to California. Every ship was jammed with people, and only by using their status as officials of the United States government did members of the boundary commission finally reach San Diego. The delay had caused them to be late for their appointment with the Mexican commission, but they found that the gold rush had delayed those officials as well.

Finally the Mexicans arrived, and introductions were made. Commanding the Mexican Boundary Commission was General

Pedro García Conde. Born in Arizpe, Sonora, in 1806, Conde had joined the Spanish army in 1818 and had served at various frontier posts. By 1828 he was a captain of engineers, and five years later he was assigned to make the first geographical map of Chihuahua. Promoted to brigadier general in 1843, he served as secretary of war and marine in the national government, and after the end of the war with the United States he was elected to the national senate. Thus Conde was an experienced frontiersman, a good engineer, and an able diplomat—not a defeated politician in need of a position from his party.

The Mexican surveyor was equally well equipped for his task. José Salazar Larregui was a native of Hermosillo, Sonora, born there in 1823. He had studied at the Colegio de Minera and had worked as an engineer in several capacities previous to 1849 and his appointment to the international survey.

On July 6, 1849, the formal work of the Joint Boundary Commission, as it was called, began. For six months thereafter they worked to survey the boundary between California and Baja California. The initial point of the boundary on the Pacific Coast was easily located, and Lieutenant Amiel W. Whipple was sent with a small party of soldiers to survey the point where the Gila and Colorado rivers joined. Despite the hordes of Forty-Niners passing through the Southwest by way of Cooke's Wagon Road, Whipple accomplished his task. It was Major Emory who devised the method of drawing the line between the initial point on the coast and the junction of the two rivers. He had gunpowder ignited at set intervals at each end of the line, and from high points of elevation in between, sightings were taken that enabled Emory to prepare an accurate map showing the longitude and latitude of the boundary at any given point in between. Then the work of running and marking this line began from both ends at the same time and when they finally came together, the two lines were only six inches apart—an error that Emory attributed to running a straight line across the curvature of the earth's surface.

The survey itself, while innovative, was not difficult, but there were political complications that hindered it. In March 1849 the

Whig administration of President Zachary Taylor assumed office in Washington, and these new officials were angry that Whigs had not been named to the offices of boundary commissioner and surveyor. They therefore began withholding funds from the Democrat Weller in order to embarrass him; without these funds Weller was unable to pay his workers, and they in turn began deserting to rush to the nearby gold fields of northern California (even some of the soldiers quietly departed without authorization, for the lure of quick riches was almost irresistible to men making only nine dollars a month).

Despite these difficulties Weller continued at his post, trying to do a good job for his country. During this part of the survey, Weller's immediate superior in Washington was the secretary of state, an office held after March 1849 by John M. Clayton. When Clayton decided that Weller was not going to resign in disgust, he wrote the commissioner on December 19 telling him that he was fired. Major Emory was to assume the duties of commissioner on a temporary basis in order to complete the survey of the boundary between Upper California and Lower California. This letter reached Weller on February 22, 1850, whereupon he departed (after California became a state that year, he ran for and was elected to the United States Senate; from this seat he kept a close watch on subsequent events).

When Weller was fired, the Joint Boundary Commission held a final meeting at which the commissioners and surveyors agreed to complete their work on the California boundary and then to meet again the following December at El Paso, Chihuahua (the present city of Juárez), there to begin surveying the eastern part of the boundary. Emory and Andrew B. Gray spent the summer of 1850 in California and did complete the marking of the boundary there before they journeyed to Washington by ship. They finally arrived in the nation's capital on November 4, 1850, where Emory asked to be relieved from any further connection with the survey; he was disgusted at the part politics was playing in the work. Gray decided to continue and was ordered to hurry to El Paso to join the commission at that point. He departed within days.

Meanwhile a new boundary commissioner had been appointed, this time one acceptable to the Whigs. Their choice was John Russell Bartlett, a native of Providence, Rhode Island. Born in 1805, he was educated in Kingston, Upper Canada, at Lowville Academy in upstate New York, and in Montreal. His schooling taught him to write a good hand, to be an accountant, and to assist his father in business; he also learned to love good books, acquired a taste for history and geography, and developed an above-average competence as an artist. In 1824, at age eighteen, he returned to Providence to clerk in a dry goods store, after which he became a bookkeeper in a bank. Also he joined the Franklin Society, the Rhode Island Historical Society, and the Providence Athenaeum. Then, after moving to New York in 1836 to open a book store with Charles Welford, he was a member of the New York Historical Society and a founder of the American Ethnological Society; this latter accomplishment grew out of his admiration for the native North American, whom he admired as Rousseau's "noble savage." And there he authored three books.

Despite his growing literary and scholarly reputation, however, Bartlett found it increasingly difficult to support his wife and four children. Thus in 1849 he journeyed to Washington with letters of introduction and a vague hope of being appointed ambassador to Denmark. He failed to win this post, but his friends did secure for him the appointment of boundary commissioner. He accepted the position, he later said, because he had never been active physically and wanted to travel, and because the job offered him a chance to see real Indians. Along with the appointment came orders to collect information on the possible construction of a road, canal, or railroad through the boundary area; to seek knowledge about quicksilver, precious metals, ores, and other such substances; to look for a more practicable route to California for immigrants; and to keep full records and make a map of the country traversed. For these services he was to receive $3000 a year plus expenses.[3]

Unfamiliar with the Southwest, ignorant of conditions there, and incapable of performing the task to which he had been appointed, Bartlett proceeded to make blunder after blunder. First

37

United States Boundary Commissioner John Russell Bartlett.
Courtesy Arizona Historical Society.

he hired an excessive number of employees, many of them the sons of prominent Whigs whose only qualification was a desire for adventure. Second, he hired his brother as commissary, but that relative used the appointment to make large sums of money for himself by purchasing poor quality food and supplies at inflated prices.

In August 1850, Bartlett, 111 civilian employees, 85 members of the 3rd Infantry serving as a military escort, mounds of equipment, and four iron boats that could be disassembled departed by ship from New York City to land at Indianola on the Texas coast. There they set out overland to reach El Paso by December 1. They ran into difficulties immediately. The harness which Bartlett's brother had purchased was designed for eastern mules and thus was two times too large for the wiry little southwestern mule. Delays followed while the harness was cut down to fit. Finally Bartlett set out in advance of the major portion of his party. His mode of conveyance was a specially built carriage which he had brought; the inside of this vehicle, according to John C. Cremony, the party's interpreter, "was well supplied with Colt's and Sharp's rifles, Colt's pistols, a double-barreled shot gun, lots of ammunition, a spyglass, and a number of small but useful tools."[4] Invariably his traveling companion in his coach was Dr. Thomas H. Webb, the surgeon and surveyor of the party and an old friend of the commissioner; the two Rhode Islanders whiled away the hours trying out their shotguns on the "prairie fowl, the great curlew, and flocks of quail."[5]

On October 5, west of the German settlement of Fredericksburg, Texas, there occurred an incident that at once demonstrated both Bartlett's ignorance about the West and his ineptitude in human relations. There he was greeted by Chipota, a fat Lipan Apache chief of some sixty winters. Bartlett received the Indian warmly but was shocked to discover that the chief primarily was interested in only one thing—a drink of whiskey. Bartlett truthfully replied that he had no alcoholic beverages, but the Indian was unconvinced; always in this region a white man politely offered an Indian a drink when the two first met. Yet Bartlett was a teetotaler as well as ignorant of local customs. The next morning, after

Plaza and church in El Paso. *From Emory, Report, I.*

Junction of the Gila and Colorado rivers.
From Bartlett, Personal Narrative, II.

spending a cold night sleeping on the ground, Chipota rapped on the window of Bartlett's sumptuous carriage, the seats of which converted into beds, and chattered through his teeth, "*Mucho frio— poco de viskey.*" (it's cold—a little whiskey). Bartlett gave him a cup of coffee. As a result the chief went away very disappointed, and he refused to sell sorely needed mules to the boundary commission.

Once the entire group arrived at El Paso, some of the young Whig gentlemen proved so incapable of performing the tasks for which they had been hired that Bartlett was forced to fire them. A few of these dandies decided to turn "Robin Hood" bandits, intending to rob from the rich in the area and give to the poor. (Local citizens who caught them did not sympathize with their good intentions and hanged them.) Moreover, the members of the commission who could do their jobs were angry at the food which Bartlett's brother had bought for them; the pork had worms in it, and the flour was filled with weevils.[6]

Bartlett's real problems started after meetings with the Mexican commissioner General Conde, began on December 3, 1850. Within weeks the American was led into a disastrous blunder. The map used to draw the boundary between the United States and Mexico at the end of the late war was a poor one; the lines of longitude and latitude were distorted, for no qualified mapmaker had ever been in the Southwest to make accurate sightings. The one the treaty-makers had used was by J. Disturnell of New York City; published in 1847, this work was a plagiarism of a map published in 1828, which in turn had been stolen from an imprint in 1826, which was a reproduction of a publication in 1822.[7] The treaty-makers at Guadalupe Hidalgo had shown the boundary turning west from the Rio Grande at a point eight miles above El Paso; their map showed El Paso to be at 32° 15′ north latitude and the Rio Grande at 104° 39′ west longitude. Lieutenant Whipple's survey showed El Paso to be at 31° 45′ and the Rio Grande at 106° 29′; this error of half a degree in latitude placed El Paso thirty-four miles too far north on the map, and the error of almost two degrees of longitude placed the Rio Grande well over a hundred miles too far east.

41

General Conde was quick to take advantage of the situation. He argued that the degrees of longitude and latitude must be used as shown on the map, regardless of the errors. The boundary, he argued, therefore should turn west from the Rio Grande forty-two miles north of El Paso, not eight as shown, and should run west three degrees from the Rio Grande *as shown on the Disturnell map* —or only to 107° 39' west longitude. In effect, General Conde was arguing that Mexico should receive an extremely large portion of territory which the treaty-makers at Guadalupe Hidalgo had not intended should be Mexican.

When Bartlett protested loudly, Conde quietly suggested a compromise. He would give way on the question of longitude if Bartlett would give way on the issue of latitude. This compromise formula would set the boundary forty-two miles north of El Paso, but the line then would run west the full three degrees of longitude before turning north to intersect the Gila. Bartlett agreed to the compromise, but Surveyor Andrew B. Gray was absent—and the signature of the Mexican and American commissioners *and* surveyors was necessary to make the agreement official. When this question arose, Bartlett appointed Lieutenant Whipple to act as American surveyor *ad interim* and ordered him to sign the agreement. This done, the commission began surveying west from the Rio Grande along what came to be known as the Bartlett-Conde Compromise line.[8]

When Andrew B. Gray finally arrived on the scene in the summer of 1851, he read the Bartlett-Conde Agreement—and refused to sign it! Instead he wrote hot letters to the secretary of the interior, who had assumed charge of the survey in Washington, and said that Bartlett's action would result in the loss of land belonging to the United States, land vitally necessary for the eventual construction of a transcontinental railroad. The tracks of such a railroad would have to run through the land Bartlett was giving to Mexico in order to avoid mountains to the north. Bartlett likewise wrote to the secretary to protest Gray's refusal to sign the agreement and to defend his own position.[9]

At this time, however, communication between El Paso and

42

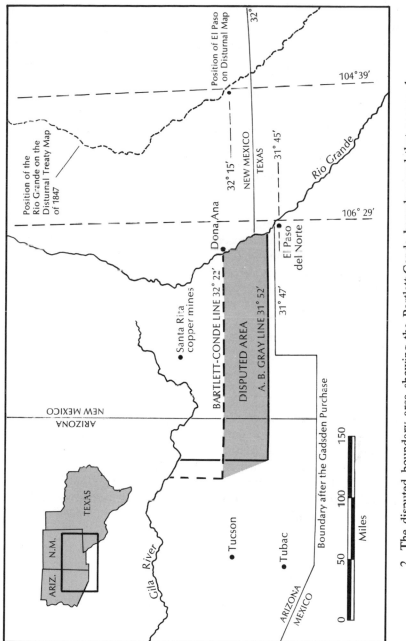

2. The disputed boundary area showing the Bartlett-Conde boundary and that proposed by A. B. Gray. *Based on a map by Don Bufkin.*

Washington was very slow. Months were necessary for letters to go from one town to the other and a reply returned. In this interval, the summer and fall of 1851, the Joint Boundary Commission decided that work could go forward on the Gila River portion of the boundary. Bartlett therefore ordered Gray, Whipple, and part of the American commission to begin this surveying; then, leaving the other part of the American commission at El Paso, Bartlett personally went south into Mexico to purchase badly needed supplies. As he departed he promised the men going to the Gila that he would rejoin them as quickly as possible. No part of the Mexican commission was able to go with the men bound for the Gila, but a small military escort of American troops was given them to protect them from raiding Indians.

These forty-seven men set to work on a task that proceeded smoothly for some 350 miles down the Gila. By December 22, however, they were so short of supplies that they decided they would have to halt the survey, although they were within sixty miles of the junction of the Gila and Colorado rivers, their goal. Their need for food was more pressing than their work, however, and they had heard nothing from the absent Commissioner Bartlett. They therefore marked with a pile of stones the spot where they halted the work and set out for San Diego, the city nearest to them; there they hoped to learn what had happened to Bartlett.

As they approached the junction of the Gila and Colorado rivers on the afternoon of December 24, 1851, these forty-seven men expected to celebrate Christmas Day in style at Camp Yuma, an army post that had been established on the California side of the Colorado. To their surprise and disappointment, however, they arrived at the river to find that Camp Yuma had been abandoned a week before.[10] Instead of food, drink, warm quarters, and a friendly welcome by fellow Americans, they were confronted by "1500 Indians, the flower of the Yuma nation." And these were angry Indians. Gray, Whipple, and the others were dismayed to find the Yumas in possession of the two flatboats used as ferries across the Colorado, for the river then was a quarter of a mile wide and from fifteen to thirty feet deep. The only way across was

44

with the help of the Yumas, but this the Indians refused to give. Moreover, during the hours of darkness that night the American interpreter overheard the natives planning to kill all the Americans.

This information naturally created a stir in the surveyors' camp. Immediately they erected a hasty breastwork of their wagons and baggage, for they intended to fight for their lives. But the next day, Christmas, passed without an attack. Perhaps it was the American preparation for battle that caused the Indians to pause.

Toward evening of Christmas Day, Chief Azul and his leading warrior, known as Juan Antonio, approached the American camp in company with their people. Because women and children were in this group, the surveyors and soldiers knew that no battle was about to start. Therefore Gray and Whipple went forward to talk with the chiefs. Azul wanted to know, through the interpreter, how much money the Americans had with them and where it was kept. Lieutenant Whipple responded that in the camp there was sufficient money to pay the Indians two dollars for each American ferried across the river and one dollar for each horse and mule.

As this conversation was taking place, the families of the chiefs came up and stood to one side. With them was a young girl of fourteen to fifteen years. Suddenly she stepped forward to whisper in the ear of her father, Juan Antonio. He in turn called Chief Azul aside and whispered to him. Other Indians wandered over to join in the mysterious conference, and when they heard what was being said they turned to look at Lieutenant Whipple. Finally Azul spoke to the interpreter, who said to Whipple, "These warriors think they have seen you before. They would like to know whether you came to the Colorado river from San Diego, on the Pacific coast, two years ago, and camped on the hill opposite this present camp."

The handsome young West Pointer replied that indeed he had been encamped there in 1849 when he had surveyed the junction of the Gila and Colorado rivers. When the interpreter conveyed this information to the Yumas, the young Indian girl arose and came forward with her father. Of this dramatic moment one American later wrote, "I saw by the expression of delight on the face of

45

Amiel W. Whipple, who worked with the boundary survey.
Courtesy Arizona Historical Society.

the interpreters that all danger was past." The reason for the Indians' change of heart soon became clear. Two years before, when Whipple had been in the area, he had come upon the young Indian "princess" lost in the desert to the west of the Colorado. She was suffering from hunger and thirst. Whipple, without considering the incident one of serious moment, had taken her to his tent where he had given her a watermelon and, as a present, a small mirror. Then he had returned her safely to her home. She had not forgotten this favor, and as a result the forty-seven Americans were spared their lives on Christmas Day of 1851. Within an hour the Yumas were ferrying them across the Colorado, even supplying them with food and guiding them across the terrible desert of southern California.[11]

Arriving at San Diego at last, late in January 1852, the party made inquiries about Commissioner Bartlett. The absent Rhode Islander finally arrived in the same city in February to say that he had found it necessary to go deep into the interior of Mexico in search of supplies which he might purchase. He had gone to Hermosillo, Sonora, and then on the Guaymas, Mazatlán, and even Acapulco. There he had taken ship for San Diego—still without acquiring the needed supplies. And once in southern California he found it necessary to take his private coach as far north as San Francisco, still in pursuit of supplies, as well as material for the book which he would write about his adventures in the West.[12] In the summer of 1852 the united group made its return trek across the Southwest, pausing to survey the last sixty miles of the Gila River. Once at El Paso they received dispatches which told how Washington officials had resolved the quarrel between Bartlett and Gray over the Bartlett-Conde Agreement. Gray had been fired![13] Whig bureaucrats were eager to protect their own appointees as the election of 1852 approached.

Replacing Gray as surveyor of the Joint Boundary Commission was Major William H. Emory. Against his will he was recalled, made surveyor, ordered to El Paso, and told to sign the Bartlett-Conde Agreement. Arriving at El Paso, the army officer found many employees of the commission idly awaiting direction; he

47

organized them and began the survey of the Rio Grande. In fact, when Bartlett finally returned to El Paso, Emory was far down-river and working steadily. Thus Bartlett and his group set out to find Emory, which they did at Christmas of 1852, after several adventures in Mexico. Emory was at Ringgold Barracks, only 241 miles from the Gulf of Mexico, and working steadily toward the Gulf.

At Ringgold Barracks, however, the survey came to an end. There Bartlett received additional dispatches from Washington, which told him to halt the survey, because Congress had cut off the funds for the work.[14] Since the early days of the survey, certain members of Congress had been watching the work of the Joint Boundary Commission and, growing increasingly unhappy, had started to try to halt the work. These congressmen did not want the Bartlett-Conde Agreement boundary to be the final dividing line between the United States and Mexico. There were millions of dollars at stake. As Andrew B. Gray had written, the 6000 square miles in dispute were vitally necessary for any future southern transcontinental railroad route. And if such a railroad was built with its eastern terminus in Louisiana or Texas, that region of the country would receive a large amount of business—and money—from the resulting traffic. Moreover, if this 6000 square miles of territory went to Mexico, the railroad probably would not have its eastern terminus in the South but in some other section of the country, which in turn would receive the material benefit.

For these reasons congressmen from Louisiana and Texas had rallied together to fight the Bartlett-Conde Agreement under a banner of patriotism: do not give to Mexico what rightfully belongs to the United States! And they were joined by ex-commissioner John B. Weller who, after being fired as head of the American commission, was elected to the United States Senate from California. He was a sharp critic of Bartlett's work. Gradually this coalition had grown in strength, so that by the summer of 1852 Bartlett stood accused of making private use of government transportation (his carriage trips to Acapulco and San Francisco), of mismanagement of government funds, of disregard for the health, comfort, and safety of the employees on the survey, and of general negligence. These charges resulted in a senatorial investigation in the summer of 1852; out of this hearing, Bartlett emerged as an inept bungler, and his agreement with General Conde was discredited.

Moreover, critics of Bartlett and his agreement were able to attach a clause to the appropriation bill fiscal year 1852-53 stating that none of the money could be spent "until it shall be made to appear to the President of the United States that the southern boundary is not established . . . further north of the town called Paso that the [line] is laid down in Disturnell's map. . . ."[15] The secretary of the interior had no recourse, after reading this proviso to the appropriations bill, but to inform Bartlett that President Millard Fillmore had concluded that the money could not legally be spent. Since all funds from prior appropriations had been expended, the secretary ordered Bartlett to make no further drafts on the United States Treasury. In short, he was to halt the survey, sell all government equipment, discharge his employees, and go home to Rhode Island.[16]

The survey thus halted—with a very inexact boundary set between the two republics and Cooke's Wagon Road yet a part of Mexico. The major question to be answered was the dividing line between the Mexican state of Chihuahua and the American territory of New Mexico: did it run eight miles or forty-two miles north of El Paso? It was a matter of 6000 square miles and was of great interest to William Carr Lane, governor of New Mexico, and to Ángel Trias, governor of Chihuahua. Governor Lane believed the land was under his jurisdiction, for he reasoned that since Andrew B. Gray had never signed the Bartlett-Conde Agreement the agreement was not binding. And to him the point was more than academic; he issued a public statement to the effect that he intended to exercise jurisdiction over the region as part of New Mexico.[17]

Governor Trias was equally determined. He asserted publicly that the Bartlett-Conde Agreement was legal and that the 6000 square miles of territory was Mexican. To ensure that he would control the area, he moved five hundred troops and six to eight pieces of artillery north toward the disputed ground, and he issued a proclamation that he would fight for the land. He found that he could not supply men that far north, however, and therefore withdrew them to El Paso. Governor Lane responded to Trias's challenge by organizing a force of New Mexican and Texan volunteers, and he likewise issued a proclamation stating his willingness to fight for the barren land. A second war between the United States and Mexico seemed about to start. Any small incident would have touched off sharp fighting, both sides believing they were in the right.[18]

At this critical juncture, however, both Mexican and American officials took a long second look at the situation. In March 1853 the newly installed President of the United States was Franklin Pierce, who knew that the first war with Mexico had badly divided the United States, and probably had caused his Democratic party to lose the election of 1848. A second war would lead to even greater losses for his party, and doubtless would divide the nation even more sharply than had the first war in 1846. In Mexico the recently installed dictator, Antonio López de Santa Anna, knew that his most pressing need was money, not a war in which victory was extremely unlikely; to stay in power he had to have "silver cannonballs," as they were called in Mexico—money to shoot to this and to that general to keep the soldiers loyal to the regime in power. Diplomacy seemed more likely to produce these funds than did battle.[19]

With such moods prevailing in Washington and in Mexico City, both governments were of a mind to remember and accede to the provisions of Article XXI of the Treaty of Guadalupe Hidalgo:

> If unhappily any disagreement should hereafter arrive between the Governments of the two Republics, whether with respect to the interpretation of any stipulation in this treaty, or with respect to any other particular concerning the political or commercial relations of the two Nations, the said Governments . . . do promise to each other, that they will endeavour in the most sincere and earnest manner, to settle the differences so arising, and to preserve the state of peace and friendship, in

which the two countries are now placing themselves; using for this end, mutual representations and pacific negotiations.[20]

President Pierce, in searching for an envoy to Mexico to discuss this difference, relied on the advice of his secretary of war, Jefferson Davis. This former senator from Mississippi and future president of the Confederate States recommended a fellow Southerner, James Gadsden. Born in Charleston, South Carolina, in 1788, Gadsden was a graduate of Yale University who had served in the army for a decade and had risen to the rank of colonel; then in 1821 he had resigned to work in Florida and then in South Carolina. In 1839 he had become president of the Louisville, Cincinnati and Charleston Railroad, a position he held for ten years. Despite the fact that this road had only a few miles of track and a $3,000,000 debt, its imposing name notwithstanding, Gadsden dreamed of consolidating the many short lines in the South into a regional system—and even building a transcontinental railroad to the Pacific Coast, one naturally with a Southern terminus. In line with this dream he was actively promoting a Gila River Route. Thus he went to Mexico with a strong desire to acquire the land necessary to the realization of his dream.

On July 15, 1853, Secretary of State William L. Marcy delivered to Gadsden a set of official instructions for negotiating a settlement of the boundary dispute, as well as all difficulties between the two nations. Primary among these was Gadsden's obligation to secure sufficient land for the building of a transcontinental railroad; for such an accommodation, the United States "would be willing to pay liberally." Should Mexico prove willing to negotiate on this score, Gadsden was not to press the American claim to the 6000 square miles of disputed territory, but if the matter became of importance he was to state that the Bartlett-Conde Agreement was illegal inasmuch as Lieutenant A. W. Whipple's signature as surveyor *ad interim* was meaningless.[21]

Gadsden's mission proved a success, for on December 30, 1853, he signed the treaty that bears his name. It set a new boundary between the two nations, one beginning at the mouth of the Rio

51

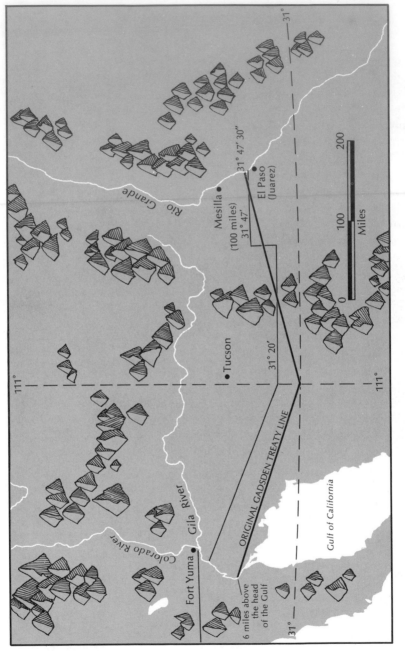

3. The original Gadsden Treaty line and the final boundary. *Based on a map by Don Bufkin.*

Grande and running up its deepest channel to 31° 47′ 30″ north latitude, thence in a straight line to the intersection of the 31st parallel with the 111th meridian, thence in another straight line to the middle of the Colorado River six miles from its mouth at the Gulf of California; from there it would go up the middle of the deepest channel of the Colorado River to its junction with the Gila, and then follow the same boundary between the two Californias, as named in the Treaty of Guadalupe Hidalgo. In return for this area, generally known as the Gadsden Purchase, the United States was to pay Mexico the sum of $15,000,000.[22]

Gadsden immediately sent this treaty to Washington. There President Pierce forwarded it to the Senate for ratification, but it quickly ran into great difficulty. One senator was so angered at the thought of the United States paying $15,000,000 for a small amount of scrubby desert land that he shouted in the senate the claim that as a private citizen he could have purchased the same area from the government of Mexico for only $6000; he said the area was fit "only for jackrabbits and coyotes." Other senators apparently agreed with this assessment, for on the first vote on the treaty it failed to receive the necessary two-thirds majority (twenty-seven favored it, with eighteen against).

Serious work then began on rewriting the treaty. First the senators cut the amount to be paid Mexico to just $10,000,000, and then they re-drew the boundary. The man most responsible for setting the final boundary between the United States and Mexico was Senator James M. Mason of Virginia; in this task he relied heavily for advice on fellow Virginian—and ex-surveyor—Andrew B. Gray. Mason did not touch the Rio Grande or the California portions of the boundary; rather it was the part separating New Mexico and Arizona from Mexico that he re drew. He set his initial point on the Rio Grande at 31° 47′ north latitude (seven miles north of El Paso), ran the boundary due west for one hundred miles, then turned it south to 31° 20′ north latitude, and then continued it due west to the 111th meridian. He made these turns because he particularly wanted to secure for the United States all of Cooke's Wagon Road, which between 1849 and 1854 had been in

53

heavy use by tens of thousands of gold-seekers bound for California.[23]

The remainder of the boundary was drawn as a result of the lobbying efforts of Juan N. Almonte, the Mexican ambassador to the United States. Almonte believed that his country could expect to lose Baja California to its northern neighbor in a few short years unless it had a usable land link between that peninsula and the rest of Mexico. Under Gadsden's original agreement, the boundary struck the Colorado River six miles above the Gulf of California, but because of the immense raising and lowering of the water when the tides ebbed and flowed—as much as forty-five feet and spreading for several miles in a wide delta—no bridge could be constructed. Almonte pled his nation's cause so effectively that the senators changed that portion of the boundary; it ran from the juncture of 31° 20′ north latitude and the 111th meridian in a straight line to a point in the middle of the Colorado just twenty miles below the California boundary.[24]

James Gadsden was so incensed at these changes in his treaty that he lobbied against its final passage, but both the United States and Mexican senates approved the document. Under this agreement, a new Joint Boundary Commission was appointed to complete the surveying of the international line. On August 15, 1854, President Pierce named Major William H. Emory to be the American commissioner *and* surveyor; by naming the same man to fill both offices the president felt he was guaranteeing that no quarrels would develop within the American half of the Joint Boundary Commission; moreover, Emory was, without doubt, the most qualified man for both posts. Emory proceeded in quick fashion to hire competent workers, bought supplies and sent them ahead, and then set out by ship for the Texas coast. He intended to meet with his Mexican counterpart, José Salazar Larregui, at El Paso during the first week of December 1854.

This sea voyage, made in September, proved stormy, for a hurricane was ravaging the Gulf of Mexico when Emory and his men neared the Texas town of Indianola aboard the *Louisiana*. Emory not only had to worry about his safety and that of his men

El Paso in 1852. *Courtesy Library of Congress.*

but also about the instruments which he had sent ahead and which he knew were stacked on the dock at Indianola to await his arrival. Somehow during that night of September 18 the captain of the *Louisiana* kept the ship afloat, and gradually the hurricane began to slacken its force. When the ship docked at Indianola a week later, Emory was greeted by a sight of terrible destruction. The town had been leveled to the ground, and every dock in the bay had been swept away—with but one exception, the one on which Emory's equipment was stacked! And Emory found, after a scientific investigation, that the storm had improved the channel leading into Matagorda Bay; it had forced the water out to sea at such a rapid rate that it had deepened the channel by two feet.[25]

That the instruments of the boundary commission had not been lost during the hurricane was an unusual stroke of good fortune for Major Emory, but he was not a man who depended on the favors of Lady Luck to make his way. Instead he relied on careful planning, based on his knowledge of surveying and of actual conditions in the field, and on his selection of the right personnel for each job. He was an excellent judge of character; the specialists he selected to collect and compile scientific information about the country along the border later would rise to the forefront among nineteenth-century scientists, men such as Dr. Charles Christopher Parry. Thus when Emory met with the Mexican boundary commission at El Paso on December 2, 1854, the work proceeded smoothly. There were no major quarrels or misunderstandings on this final part of the survey. There were no drunkards running an incorrect boundary, or even men so thirsty that they surveyed a line to the nearest town where they could buy a beer.

Emory divided his men into two parties, one to work under his personal direction westward from El Paso, and the other he sent under Lieutenant Nathaniel Michler to Fort Yuma to survey the Colorado River and the leg of the boundary running from there to the 111th meridian. The two groups met on August 16, 1855, the field work complete (for the California and Rio Grande portions had already been completed under the old treaty). Emory and Salazar held their final meeting to sign a statement certifying that the entire boundary had been surveyed correctly and that appropriate boundary markers had been set in place all along the new line. A boundary finally had been set between the two republics, and it had been surveyed.

His work in the field done, Emory returned to Washington, where he busied himself in the next two years preparing a full report of his work for publication. Half of this was printed in 1857, and two years later the other half appeared in two volumes. The satisfactory completion of this task brought such distinction to Major Emory that he was promoted to lieutenant colonel. More than this, however, Emory's *Report of the United States and Mexican Boundary Survey* contained the first really accurate maps of the Southwest and of Cooke's Wagon Road, along with excellent descriptions, and often pictures, of conditions, plants, and animals of the region.

The maps did not appear in print in time to be of service to the first major horde of pilgrims to use this overland route, the gold-seekers of Forty-Nine. While Cooke's Wagon Road was influencing the final boundary between the United States and Mexico, an abstract line upon the surface of the earth, it was being put to hard and practical use by thousands and tens of thousands of Americans who considered themselves far more practical than the government servants trying to survey and mark the international boundary. The lure of quick riches was a powerful magnet to eastern men, one that lured them across Cooke's Wagon Road even in the absence of good maps.

3

Travelers on the Trail

Young Benjamin Butler Harris was strongly aware of his thirst as he rode his tired horse in a southwesterly direction early in May of 1849. He was almost four hundred miles west of the last frontier shack in Texas, and he had ridden seventy miles since crossing the Concho River, the last place he had been able to get water. The spring rains had not come often that year, so all the waterholes and springs were dry; moreover, the day was unusually hot for that time of year. The sun had already burned the western Texas area and it looked like the end of summer. Harris knew he was riding along the Great Comanche War Trail; that should lead him to water soon, for the Indians had to quench their thirst just as did Harris and his horse.

Suddenly the tired animal lifted his head and broke into a trot. The rider did not try to slow the beast, little caring whether it had been frightened by the smell of Indians on the warpath or if it scented wild horses in the vicinity. His thirst was a strong craving that gnawed at his insides until nothing else mattered. In fact, he did not see the Pecos River ahead until it was just yards away. Then, even if he had wanted, he could not have halted the thirst-mad horse. Over the bank tumbled man and animal, falling into water that was more than twenty feet deep and flowing at a good speed. Slipping from his saddle, Harris made no attempt to get ashore but did hold lightly to the saddle in which he had sat for so long. He and the horse drifted half a mile downstream as they drank their fill. Finally, their thirst quenched, they climbed the embankment. There Harris filled his canteen, then mounted his dripping horse and rode back along his route to tell the fifty-one others in his party that water was ahead.

Left. Benjamin B. Harris.
Courtesy Library of Congress.

Below. Crossing the Pecos River.
From A. B. Gray,
Survey of a Route for the
Southern Pacific Railroad (1856).

Once at the Pecos, the remaining members of the party, like Harris before them, drank their fill. Then they crossed the wide stream on makeshift rafts. Safely on the west bank, these gold-seekers decided to camp for a few days to rest and refresh themselves and their jaded animals. Antelope and buffalo were numerous in the area, and fresh meat along with the wild onions they found growing in the vicinity were a welcome supplement to their usual diet of fried salt pork, dry beans, and strong coffee.[1]

The group, which was led by Isaac H. Duval, was one of the first to travel overland to California by way of Cooke's Wagon Road after news of the discovery of gold had spread across the United States. Departing eastern Texas on March 25, 1849, the fifty-two men pushed westward to the Brazos River, and then they made the long, dry trek toward the Pecos River. This journey they made with almost no knowledge of actual conditions along what they would call the Gila Trail, although in reality the road from New Mexico westward to California was the route pioneered by the Mormons under Lieutenant Colonel Philip St. George Cooke. Besides the usual pistols and rifles, they were armed with the courage of ignorance. They little realized the danger of the desert. Once they reached the Pecos, however, they began to learn.

One afternoon, as the members of this party were lazily swimming in the Pecos, a group of fast-moving riders approached from the west. Plainly in sight at the head of these newcomers were Indians. The men in the Duval party rushed from the river to their camp, grabbed their rifles, and turned to make a stand, still dripping naked. Their fear was natural, for they had been warned of possible Indian attacks in the region of the Pecos; one frontiersman in the last settlement to the east had told them, "Shoot at every Indian you see and save them from a life of misery. . . ." With such an attitude prevailing among the whites, the natives naturally were hostile, and warfare was common between the two races.

In that last second before members of the Duval party squeezed their triggers, they saw Americans in the on-coming party. Guns then were lowered, and fear was replaced by laughter as the California-bound group sought clothing to cover their nakedness.

The newcomers were not members of a war party of Comanches looking for scalps but were explorers commanded by Major Robert S. Neighbors and Texas Ranger Captain John S. "Rip" Ford. Their charge toward the river stemmed not from any desire to scare the Forty-Niners, but rather from the same source as Harris's earlier run: they and their horses were thirsty. And the Neighbors-Ford expedition gladly accepted an invitation to eat with the Duval party, for they had been reduced to living on mule meat at the time they crossed the plains eastward from El Paso. Their supplies had run out, and they had been unable to find game.

And as the two parties talked, they discovered that they were at the Pecos River that May of 1849 for the same reason—the gold rush—but with different goals. The Duval group was bound for California and the diggings, hoping to get rich, while the Neighbors-Ford party was trying to open a wagon road from San Antonio to El Paso so that gold-seekers could travel safely westward across Texas to a point where they could get on Cooke's Wagon Road, a known route from the vicinity of El Paso to the west.

And there were thousands of other individuals, in addition to those in the Duval party, trying to reach California that spring of 1849. The whole country was infected with the same desire as a result of a chance discovery some sixteen months earlier in the Sacramento Valley of California. In January 1848 James W. Marshall was supervising the construction of a sawmill for his employer, John A. Sutter. On the morning of January 24, while inspecting progress on the digging of the tailrace, through which water would run to turn the mill wheel, Marshall noticed the glint of metal in the bottom of the stream. Some of these flakes he picked up and put in the dented crown of his slouch hat, then ran to the mill shouting, "Boy, I believe I've found a gold mine." At first he thought this a good joke.

At the mill site Marshall tried every way he knew to determine if the metal he had found actually was gold and not some other type of metal. Unable to tell for certain, he took samples of it to his employer, and together they tried every test on the metal which the *American Encyclopedia* suggested. At last they became convinced

61

that indeed they had discovered gold. Yet Sutter was not at all happy with this find, for he realized that news of a gold discovery on his property would bring a rush of people whom he could not possibly keep away. They would overrun his property, destroy his crops, kill his cattle, and possibly steal his land.[2] But such news could not be kept from spreading. In May that same year an energetic San Francisco businessman and Mormon elder named Sam Brannan returned to his home city after a trip to Sutter's property. Brannan walked down the streets of San Francisco holding aloft a quinine bottle full of gold dust and bellowed, "Gold! Gold! Gold from the American River." The result was electric.

Within days shopkeepers in San Francisco hung signs on their doors proclaiming, "Gone to the Diggings." Schools closed as teachers and pupils alike abandoned books and studies. San Francisco almost became a ghost town, as did Monterey, Santa Barbara, Los Angeles, San Diego, and other California settlements. Soldiers deserted their posts, sailors abandoned ships, lawyers left their clients, and editors quit publishing their newspapers. Before the end of 1848 gold-seekers already were arriving from Hawaii, Mexico, British Columbia, South America, and even far-off Australia.

Stories of this discovery gradually drifted to the eastern United States, but most people thought these were just rumor or else dismissed them as too fantastic for belief—and by the time these stories had been repeated several times, they did defy belief. Yet in December 1848 the stories were declared true when President James K. Polk included official dispatches from California in his last annual message to Congress. Said the president, "The accounts of the abundance of gold in that territory are of such an extraordinary character as would scarcely command belief were they not corroborated by the authentic reports of officers in the public service."

Two days later a government courier arrived in Washington with a tea caddy full of gold—and all sanity, along with any lingering doubts, vanished from the public mind. That tea caddy did for the East what Sam Brannan's quinine bottle had done for San Francisco. The New York *Herald,* in a special edition, commented,

". . . Husbands are preparing to leave their wives, sons are parting with their mothers, and bachelors are abandoning their comforts; all are rushing head over heels toward the El Dorado on the Pacific." Wherever and whenever men congregated that winter of 1848-49, the talk was of California and the gold strike. The stories and rumors grew with each telling until most people believed that large chunks of gold were just laying on the ground waiting for some pilgrim to come along and pick them up. By the spring of 1849 tens of thousands of eastern Americans were ready to depart for the gold fields to do the picking up.

These Forty-Niners, as they were called, used four principal routes to get to their destination, two by land and two by sea. Those people near the Atlantic seaboard naturally chose the water routes, the first of which was around South America. This was an 18,000-mile voyage of some six to eight months, a long and tedious trip for excited gold-seekers; nevertheless in just that one year of 1849 some 15,000 chose this method of travel.

The second water route involved a divided voyage by way of Panama. The pilgrim took ship from the East Coast to the Isthmus. There he got aboard a canoe for a trip up the Chagres River and then made an overland trek through treacherous jungle. The native guides, who supplied canoes and pack animals, often were thieving, their prices too high, their tempers and actions unpredictable. Cholera, dysentery, and yellow fever took a heavy toll of Forty-Niners on this route. And at Panama City, on the Pacific Coast, the gold-seeker usually had to wait weeks and even months before he was able to secure passage on a ship bound for California. Too many sailors abandoned their ships at San Francisco, for they were eager to get to the goldfields themselves rather than return to Panama to ferry the emigrants out to get the gold.

The most popular way to California for Americans, however, was overland. For those people living in the Midwest and the Mississippi Valley, the easiest route was one known as the Humboldt Trail. This trail, pioneered by fur traders and trappers, began in Missouri, went up the Missouri River to the Platte, followed the Platte to its source near South Pass, then moved by various trails

63

across the Great Basin, and labored through narrow mountain passes in the Sierra to the Pacific slope. A wagon and oxen, sufficient food, and a few tools were all a man needed to begin this trek —in addition to sufficient optimism to abandon home—and the average farmer had all these. Some 45,000 Forty-Niners used the Humboldt Trail that first year of the run to California.

Other gold-seekers, especially Southerners, chose to go west by Cooke's Wagon Road, or, as it became known, the Gila Trail. Even some Midwesterners chose this route, for they could follow the Santa Fe Trail from Missouri to New Mexico and there find the wagon tracks left by the Mormon Battalion. From the southern states, a Forty-Niner would travel well-established roads into Arkansas, Louisiana, or Texas. The towns in these states, such as Fort Smith, New Orleans, Shreveport, San Antonio, Corpus Christi, and even Brownsville, actively promoted the Gila Trail, for the residents in these towns believed they would get rich from selling supplies to the pilgrim bound for California, who had to purchase food for himself and for his animals before he embarked on the trail.[3]

Moreover, the city that built a reputation for itself as the jumping-off point for western travel might reap more substantial rewards, for already there was much talk about building a transcontinental railroad—the eastern terminus of which would become a major city. Thus each town promoted itself and its local road, and newspapers in each painted glowing word pictures about the Gila Trail and the best way to get to it. The editor of the Houston *Democratic Telegraph and Register* in his issue of March 8, 1849, noted the quarrels thus engendered:

> The editors of the Port Lavaca Journal, Victoria Advocate, Western Texian at Bexar, the Corpus Christi Star, and Brownsville Flag, are engaged in a very profitless discussion respecting the advantages of the routes from each of these places to California. Some of the editors in New Orleans have taken sides with the Corpus Christi paper, and the Crescent actually published a map, delineating a route from Corpus Christi, which leads, no honest man in Texas can say where, for it has never been explored. . . .

San Antonio in the 1850s. *From Emory, Report, I.*

Businessmen similarly engaged in the quarrel by bearing the expense of printing brochures and pamphlets promoting their own town above all others.

Just as newspaper editors and businessmen's pamphlets promoted various approaches to the Gila Trail, so also were there individuals trying to have good approach roads opened to New Mexico. Many cities were not situated directly on a well-defined road, but the surveying and mapping of a road nearby would make it accessible and traffic would increase quickly. For example, businessmen in Austin, with an eye to profiting from this traffic, masterminded the Neighbors-Ford expedition of 1849, the one that met the Duval party on the lonely banks of the Pecos River. That effort was jointly sponsored by the federal government, which felt the need of a military road between San Antonio and El Paso, and these citizens of Austin, Texas.

Neighbors and Ford departed San Antonio on March 23, 1849, heading in a northwesterly direction. At the headwaters of the Concho River, they turned toward Horsehead Crossing of the Pecos, and arrived at El Paso on May 2. Pausing only for a brief rest, they and their men started homeward on May 6 and encountered the Duval party at the Pecos later that month. The two groups separated after a short visit, the gold-seekers going on to California[4] and the Neighbors-Ford party proceeding to San Antonio, where it arrived on June 2. Neighbors and Ford reported to their respective bosses that their expedition was a success, both soldier and civilian swearing that theirs was an excellent wagon road.[5] Soon maps were being circulated in the East by Austin businessmen; they showed the pilgrim how to get from Austin to El Paso and Cooke's Wagon Road—presumably after making many purchases in the capital city of Texas.

Simultaneous with this search for a southern wagon road, another expedition was exploring a route usable by wagons, this one from Fort Smith, Arkansas, to Santa Fe, New Mexico. Fort Smith and nearby Van Buren were contesting for supremacy in this trade, the prize the money that Forty-Niners would spend in the town gaining the best reputation as a jumping-off place for California.

Colonel John S. "Rip" Ford.
Courtesy Western History Collections, University of Oklahoma Library.

Randolph B. Marcy when he had attained the rank of general.
Courtesy Western History Collections, University of Oklahoma Library.

Residents of Fort Smith late in 1848 called on General Matthew Arbuckle, commander of the army post at Fort Smith, to win his support for a road from their town to Santa Fe, for they hoped the road would be opened at military expense. When General Arbuckle indicated his approval, local residents then went before the state legislature to solicit its support, and that body duly petitioned the secretary of war to authorize a military expedition to open a wagon road along the Red River from Fort Smith westward to Santa Fe. Late in February 1849 Congress appropriated $50,000 for various surveys from the Mississippi River to the Pacific Coast, the Fort Smith route to be one of them.

Some 2000 immigrants gathered at Fort Smith that spring to take advantage of a military escort across the Indian-infested plains. Commanding the infantry and dragoon troops assigned to this chore was Captain Randolph B. Marcy. Soldiers and civilians departed on April 4. For more than a hundred miles these pilgrims fought their way through a sea of mud that had resulted from heavy rains in February and March that year. At last they came to firmer ground as they followed the Canadian River westward. They walked up the river, then crossed over the high plains into eastern New Mexico to arrive safely at Santa Fe on June 28. In eighty-five days they had walked 819.5 miles. Marcy computed that in the 65 days actually devoted to travel they had averaged 13 miles a day. On his return trip, made without the hindrance of civilians, Marcy chose to try a different route; he went down the Rio Grande to the town of Dona Ana, traveled east to the Pecos River, went across northwest Texas and southern Oklahoma, and arrived safely at Fort Smith. This lower road became known as Marcy's Trail in honor of the man who opened it.[6]

Marcy's journal was published in 1850, but newspapers in Arkansas and in other parts of the country spread word of his accomplishment within weeks after his return to Fort Smith on November 19, 1849. They advertised Marcy's Road as the shortest and fastest way to California, and the resulting traffic proved a boon to merchants in Arkansas; Forty-Niners passing through the state purchased foodstuff such as dried fruit, coffee, flour, and salt pork along with personal needs such as clothing, bedding, cooking utensils, rifles, pistols, and ammunition.

Residents of Van Buren were furious that Fort Smith had edged them out in the race for this traffic. The victory was even sweeter for residents of Fort Smith because the federal government had paid for the effort. No matter how much these townsmen might quarrel among themselves as to which was the best jumping-off point and which was the best road to New Mexico, all of them agreed that from New Mexico westward the Gila Trail was far superior to the Humboldt or any other route to California. And the Gila Trail did have some attractive features. It crossed fewer mountains than the trails to the north did, and the weather on the Gila Trail, although hot, was more tolerable than the summer sun and wintry cold along the Humboldt Trail. Also, there were several towns along the way, some of them across the line in Chihuahua and Sonora, where food and other supplies could be purchased: clothing, rope, corn, barley, eggs, dried beef, and, as one pilgrim wrote, "miserable coffee."

At the embarkation towns in Texas, Arkansas, and Missouri, the gold-seekers would gather in large numbers early in the spring, waiting for the grass to grow along the trail to a height that would feed their stock. Because these pilgrims knew so little about sanitation, these gathering points became hotbeds of sickness. They drank brackish water, which they often dipped from the same place they bathed, washed their clothes, and dumped their wastes. The arrival of spring heat, coupled with these primitive sanitary conditions, too frequently was the herald for an outbreak of some epidemic of sickness. Cholera proved the most deadly, striking at San Antonio, Laredo, and Brownsville in the spring of 1849. In fact, at San Antonio that year General William J. Worth reported that so many people had died that no one bothered to ring the cathedral bells anymore, that even brave men were fearful for their lives, and that many were fleeing the city to the country.

Such outbreaks of sickness caused some wagon trains to leave earlier than had been intended, while others would not begin rolling until later in the season. When these wagon trains finally did arrive in New Mexico, either by way of the Santa Fe Trail from Missouri, Marcy's Trail from Arkansas, or one of the several routes across Texas, they then pushed on to the Gila Trail to take them across southern New Mexico and Arizona to California. Those who had thought the difficulties of Texas, Arkansas, Missouri, Kansas, or Oklahoma were terrible would look back later on this part of the trek as the most pleasant time of the journey—especially when they came to the rigors of the full desert in western Arizona and southeastern California.

In fact, the particular stretch from Tucson to San Diego proved so hard that it brought out the worst in some individuals and, on occasion, inventiveness in others. For example, one party of pilgrims, who had styled themselves the Peoria Company, arrived at the Pima villages at the junction of the Santa Cruz and Gila rivers 105 miles north of Tucson to find their earlier unity falling apart; the rigors of the desert had ended the friendship with which the group had begun. Some of the members of the company had horses and mules yet in good shape, while the animals of most of the other people were jaded. Those with good beasts wanted to hurry ahead to the gold fields. Another group, all members of the Masonic order, set up a tent and held a secret meeting at which they decided to abandon their slower companions. Yet another faction consisted of two men without horses; they put their possessions into packs and set out walking for Yuma carrying eighty-five pounds on their backs. Eventually all that was left, according to Charles E. Pancoast, a Quaker member of the company, was the "Crippled Ducks."

These people decided, as they watched the others disappear to the west, that without animals to pull their wagons they had but one choice: they would make rafts from their wagons and let the current of the Gila River move them to Yuma. As the Pima Indians watched in curiosity, the "Crippled Ducks" took their wagons apart to build two crude rafts that even included on one of them a small shed to provide protection for one Missourian's pregnant wife. On November 5, 1849, they cast off using makeshift oars and stone anchors. They arrived at Yuma six days before the members of the

71

Travelers on the plains. *From Harper's Weekly.*

Cultivated fields of the Pima Indians. *From John Bartlett, Personal Narrative, II.*

company who were traveling in wagons. And on the way the pregnant woman gave bith to a daughter who reportedly was given the name "Gila."[7]

Because most of these wagon trains of Forty-Niners were large, they were not bothered by the Indians as they crossed the Southwest. In fact, the Pima Indians of central Arizona saved many lives, not only by selling food to hungry pilgrims but also through various acts of kindness. Many of the gold-seekers would write later of the generosity of this tribe. However, the women who made this trip were terrified by stories of horrible events. And their children would squeal with delight when they saw genuine natives.

There was some reason to fear the Indians of the Southwest, especially the Apaches, but the causes of any hostility were not peculiar to either race. The mountain men, who usually served as guides for these parties of pilgrims bound west by wagon train, knew that in large numbers there was safety and would tell the women and children—along with some of the men—that they had nothing to fear. And generally the Indians were friendly toward Americans in the years just after the war with Mexico; these natives had been raiding in Mexico for years and were sworn enemies of Mexicans, while the first Americans to enter the area came in 1846 likewise to fight the Mexicans. Yet the Indians of the Southwest would sometimes attack individual or small groups of Americans foolish enough to try to cross the region; such attacks came because the Indian lived by raiding, not because they hated Americans.

An example of this type of raid was the one on the Oatman family in 1850. In January that year the Oatmans arrived in Tucson in company with a large wagon train. Most of the others voted to stay a few days in that city to rest, but three families, including the Oatmans, chose to push on, for they were in a hurry to reach California. The party arrived at the Pima villages on the Gila River on February 16 and stopped there to purchase supplies. The other two families decided they would wait at the villages until a wagon train came along; the additional people would provide safety in numbers for the remainder of the trip, much of which was across Indian country. The Oatmans decided to go on alone. On the evening of

73

March 19, the family encamped on the banks of the Gila some 118 miles east of Yuma. That evening the father was depressed and said to his wife and children, "I know something dreadful is about to happen."

He was right. Early the next morning nineteen Yavapai Indians rode up demanding food from the Oatmans. The father truthfully told them that he had little food. The Indians talked for a while, doubtless waiting to see if any other wagons might come over the horizon. Finally satisfied that the Oatmans indeed were alone, the Yavapais attacked. With their war clubs they killed Oatman, his wife, and their three youngest children. Lorenzo, an older boy, was clubbed and thrown over a cliff for dead, while Olive Oatman, age twelve, and Mary, age eight, were made captives. Lorenzo later recovered consciousness, was picked up by a passing wagon train after wandering in the desert for many hours, and was taken to Fort Yuma, the army post on the California side of the Colorado River that had been established late in 1849 to protect the gold-seekers. At Fort Yuma, Lorenzo tried to get the soldiers to attempt the recovery of his sisters, whom he knew to be alive because their bodies had not been found at the wagon, but the troops were too few in number even to try. Lorenzo moved to Los Angeles at last, and there for five years he sought aid in the rescue of his sisters.

Meanwhile Olive and Mary were traded to the Mohave Indians. Young Mary was unable to eat Indian foods, and the shock of her family's death caused her gradually to pine away until she died. Olive was not well but she was able to stay alive. She was tattooed in Mohave fashion and forced to do slave labor. Later she was given to a Mohave family that treated her in better fashion. She regained her health and waited for the rescue that she hoped would come someday.

Finally in January of 1856 Henry Grinnell, a carpenter at Fort Yuma, heard of the female captive of the Mohaves; Francisco, a Yuma Indian, told him that up the Colorado River a white girl was being held by these natives. Grinnell acted as if he knew about the captive girl. Immediately he picked up a Los Angeles newspaper and, pretending to read from it, made up a story to the effect that a large party of armed Americans were coming from California to kill all the Mohaves for holding the girl. Francisco was much interested in Grinnell's comment that a large reward would go to anyone who rescued Olive Oatman. He asked about this, and Grinnell promised him warm blankets, many trinkets, and much food. The Yuma warrior thereupon promised that he would go to the Mohave villages and return to Fort Yuma with the girl—which he did.

Francisco secured Olive's release by trading a few trinkets and some cloth to the Mohaves for her, and by making them believe that shortly they would all be killed if they did not release her. As Francisco was taking Olive toward Fort Yuma, however, the Mohaves changed their minds and pursued Francisco, but he was able to make his escape and bring the girl safely to the army post. For several days the girl, seventeen years old, was unable to speak. English words gradually began coming back to her, and haltingly she told of her five years of captivity among the Indians. Lorenzo, when located and told of his sister's rescue, made a quick ride across the desert of southern California for a tearful reunion with Olive. Later they moved to Oregon, where Olive was educated and then married.[8]

The Oatman family thus paid a heavy price for its ignorance of conditions in the Southwest. Other families and individuals were more fortunate, although no less ignorant. Lieutenant Cave J. Couts, who commanded the small escort of soldiers sent to protect Lieutenant Amiel W. Whipple and the boundary surveyors who were at Yuma Crossing in the fall of 1849 (before Fort Yuma was established), wrote in his journal of the hunger and ignorance of the gold-seekers then plodding across the desert; "Oh God! when will I get out of this snap, trouble, vexation, pain, suffering and annoyance, from North, South, East and West . . . ," he wrote in his diary. "This is the first leisure hour, now 10 at night, that I have had since the 12th and there is now a multitude of women and children, on the opposite bank, sending me word that they will be over to see me tomorrow!"[9]

They came in such numbers to see Couts for two reasons: they needed directions, and they were very, very hungry. Couts noted

75

Olive Oatman, who spent five years as an Indian slave.
(Note the Mohave tatoos on her chin.)
Courtesy Arizona Historical Society.

their need for food by saying that on the evening he was writing he had been able to eat by himself for the first time in two weeks. A soft-hearted and kind man, he could not turn these hungry pilgrims away. "My table admits of but three seats, and upon several occasions, I have not got in before the 4th table, very frequently having to keep it set from three p.m., until eight or nine o'clock at night, and then direct the cook to say that the provisions are out, and that the commissary Sergt. is absent," he wrote. It was difficult for him to eat while listening to the pleas of starving Forty-Niners, and they came all day every day: "From the way they shovel down the pork and bread, is sufficient proof of its rarity, and sugar and coffee! Some are worse than ratholes to fill." When he did invite them to eat, they tried to eat their fill!

As soon as these pilgrims finished the meal provided by Couts and his cook, they then wanted him to draw them maps of the route across southern California. By the time they had reached Yuma, these gold-seekers no longer were so confident of their ability to travel an unknown land; Couts had come across from San Diego, and thus, as he wrote, "They . . . are willing to keep me talking and making way-bills [maps] for them from sun-up until sun-down and from sun-down to sun-up. In addition to this they beg me for rations day in and day out."[10]

Ignorance, hunger, heat, disease, desert, Indian danger—none of these stopped the Forty-Niners from crossing the Southwest over Cooke's Wagon Road. But some of these tourists on what they called the Gila Trail more than repaid the Indians for their few raids on American parties. In fact, a few of the more adventurous "Argonauts" chose to work their way west by becoming scalp bounty hunters for the governments of the Mexican states of Chihuahua and Sonora. In 1849 these bounties were attractive to someone who did not mind killing Indians: $200 for the scalp of warrior and $100 for the scalp of a woman or child. Prominent among those who engaged in this "backyard barbering" were Michael James Box, James Kirker, James Johnson, and John Joel Glanton. These men and their followers would go into the village of some group of Indians and kill every man, woman, and child; then the

77

bodies would be scalped and the hair turned into examining committees in Chihuahua or Sonora for payment of the grisly reward.

On occasion it happened that the scalp bounty hunter went too far in his bloody quest for hair. He found that it was impossible for the examining committees to tell the difference between the scalp of a friendly Indian and that of an unfriendly Indian, and by his actions he soon had the entire Southwest aflame and all natives turned against Americans. Moreover, the scalp-hunter learned that the examining committees could not tell the difference between Indian hair and Mexican hair, and he was soon raiding remote Mexican villages, where he killed everyone in his mad search for "hairy banknotes." Such a man was John Joel Glanton.

Glanton was operating first in the state of Chihuahua, but he had to flee westward when it was discovered he was turning in the hair of Mexicans for bounty money. With a price of $8000 on his own long, snakey locks, offered by the government of Chihuahua, Glanton moved his band of cutthroats to Sonora. One pass through the countryside there netted them more than $6500 in bounty money, but again Glanton found it necessary to move on and went to Arizona. At Yuma Crossing on the Gila Trail, he and his men found the Yuma Indians profitably operating a ferry service for travelers on the Gila Trail. Glanton and his gang saw the potential of this operation, and since Fort Yuma was at this time abandoned there were no soldiers in the area to prevent their taking the ferry by force. Soon the gang was happily robbing both those going to the gold fields and those returning from them. The Yuma Indians suffered their loss in silence for a time; then on April 23, 1850, they attacked Glanton and his men and killed fifteen of them in retaking their property. Among the dead was Glanton. He had been scalped.[11]

A few survivors from Glanton's gang made their way to Los Angeles, where they complained of a "Yuma massacre" of innocent businessmen. The state of California that fall of 1850 responded by sending an expedition of volunteers to punish the Yumas. However, the Indians easily defeated these citizen-soldiers, who returned to the coast without further ado.

78

Also trekking across the Gila Trail toward California during these years were cattlemen from Texas. They were not traveling to search for gold but rather to get high prices for their animals. The quick growth of population in California during the years 1848-53 had caused the ranchers in that region to sell most of their cattle; animals that had gone for only $5 or $6 a head suddenly fetched as much as $500 apiece on the hoof in the gold camps, where hungry miners were willing to pay almost any price for a steak. And when California ranchers could no longer supply this demand, drovers from far-off Texas hurried to take advantage of the prices.

The first herd to make this long walk was from Washington County, Texas. In 1848, T. J. Trimmer took 500 head across the Southwest by way of the Gila Trail and received $100 apiece for his effort. When he returned to Texas to tell what was being paid in California for cattle, the stampede was on. Other ranchers wanted to get part of the profits, and they began driving longhorn cattle westward.

The longhorn proved an ideal animal for trailing across the arid Southwest. It could walk 60 miles without a drink. In addition, it had great stamina and endurance. But the quality of the beef taken from this animal was poor; usually it was tough and stringy. Because of the need for meat in the gold camps, however, the miners ate longhorn meat happily; they paid the high prices without complaining—and the long sinuous line of longhorns continued to move westward out of Texas and across Cooke's Wagon Road to California. Even as T. J. Trimmer returned to Texas early in 1849, he met another herd on the way. And at Fredericksburg, Texas, that same year, another large herd was gathered; when it departed for California, it had "three or four thousand horses and mules . . . besides numerous herds of cattle." Almost overnight Houston and San Antonio became jumping-off places for this trade. Both cities profited handsomely from the cattle drives to California, for the cowboys, like the other travelers, needed food and supplies.

Nor did the trade end quickly. As late as the spring of 1854 John Hames, a frontiersman, surveyor, and cattleman, gathered a herd and departed for the golden West. One of his cowhands,

79

twenty-two-year-old James G. Bell, kept a diary during the drive. Bell described the towns he saw along the way, as well as noting the changes in geography, the animals he saw, and the day-to-day routine of trail-driving. Of Tucson, the major city on the Gila Trail, he commented that Mexican soldiers were still there despite the Gadsden Purchase having made southern Arizona a part of the United States (the Mexican soldiers would remain in the fort at Tucson until March 1856); but that army did not impress the young cowboy. He wrote of them, "The Military, what shall I say of them? Their appearance twice a day, at morning and evening parade, is well calculated to keep one fat; or kill him; for if a certain amount of laughter will keep one fat, a greater amount would have the latter effect." What made him laugh so hard at the Mexican soldiers was the fact that "it is difficult to distinguish the soldiers from the citizens, and can only be done so by the difference in ornament. Each soldier has an ornament stuck on some part of the body, without regard to fitness. They are in fact a set of *ragmuffins*."[12]

Tucson and the Mexican citizens did not impress the Texans, but no record survives to tell what the Mexicans thought of the trail drivers from the Lone Star State. Yet it was the gold-seekers and the Texas cowboys who were the wave of the future, not the Mexicans who represented the past 300 years of history. Those Texas longhorns parading through the streets of Tucson and the bearded prospectors who had gone before them were Arizona's future, which would be in mining and ranching. It was they who would make use of Arizona's minerals and Arizona's grass, just as they would in New Mexico and California.

Some of the prospectors who rushed to California did get rich, but not very many of them. Most found gold-seeking to be monotonous and backbreaking. Often these miners stood for hours waist deep in icy streams, laboring day by day for the precious yellow grains of "dust." At night they returned to shacks, lean-tos, even caves to eat uninviting meals of coffee, beans, and greasy pork. And the "cities" that sprang into existence nearby to sell them goods and entertainment were only slightly more comfortable. The buildings in these towns, even those boasting populations in the thousands, were constructed of juniper posts, willow branches, blankets, and rawhide. Shacks dotted the streets, which dodged at acute angles or struggled up the sides of mountains. The restaurant might be roofless, the walls made of flour sacks the tables of rough planks, and the floors of mud. And what names these settlements had— Whiskey Bar, Skunk Gulch, Hell's Delight.

Men living under such conditions thought longingly of home, of loved ones and friends left behind. How they longed for mail to hear of marriages and births—even of deaths. One old miner in California summed up his own situation by stating, "There's nothing to do here but hang around the saloons, get drunk and fight, and lie out in the snow and die."[13] To men such as this, a letter from home became more meaningful than anything else was. For this reason they brought pressure to bear on their government at all levels to improve the mail service between the "states" and California, while those who did strike it rich wanted stagecoach transportation eastward for themselves or else stagecoach transportation westward for their families.

Thus the chance discovery of gold in California had made Cooke's Wagon Road, now called the Gila Trail, a major artery of westward migration; once the rush was over, that same gold rush made the Gila Trail an artery of travel and communication between California and the rest of the Union. How the Gila Trail functioned as an artery of transportation and communication affected the destiny of the entire Southwest.

4

The Overland Mail

Alexander Todd, an obscure Forty-Niner, profited from the wealth available to anyone who could move mail and passengers in California in the early 1850s. Todd was at the diggings upriver from San Francisco when he decided he would return to his home in the East. Publicly he announced that he would carry mail out to the nearest post office for the price of one ounce of gold dust per letter —and so eager were the miners to communicate with the outside world that Todd had more than one hundred customers for his private mail service for only a hundred miles.

Next, Todd purchased a crude raft on which to make his trip downstream. Needing help in manning the oars, he advertised that he would carry passengers downriver to Sacramento for sixteen dollars a head, and that those who paid this exorbitant sum also would have to help row the craft. So pressing was the demand for transportation that Todd soon filled the craft; in one endeavor alone he took in more than twice what he paid for the ungainly skiff.

Todd's enterprise illustrates how eager the newcomers to California were for communication with the East and for transportation of any kind. A quarter of a million men and more had rushed west during the bonanza years of 1849-53, most of them leaving their wives, sweethearts, children, parents, and other relatives behind. Some of these newcomers wanted to return home, either with the riches they had found or else in disgust at not getting the nuggets they had expected. Others of them wanted to bring their families west to settle permanently in the new state on the Pacific Coast. And all wanted some way to communicate other than the slow method of sending letters by sea; in 1848 the Post Office Department had awarded contracts for a semi-monthly service by sea be-

A stagecoach taking "girls" to the mining camps in California.
From Harper's Weekly.

tween New York and San Francisco, under the terms of which the United States Steamship Company carried the mail to Panama, it then traveled overland to Panama City, and finally was carried to California on the ships of the Pacific Mail Steamship Company. This trip was supposed to be made in thirty days, but usually took longer, with the cost varying from twelve to eighty cents per ounce.

Congressional leaders and national politicians were aware of the voters' demand for a better means of travel and communication between East and West, just as they knew businessmen wanted a means of transporting freight to ports on the Pacific in order to gain access to the Oriental trade. And by the early 1850s the railroad had proven that it was the best means for moving both people and goods. The technical experts believed that it would take just ten days to go from the East Coast to the West Coast.

One proponent of a transcontinental railroad was Asa Whitney, a merchant in New York City who was engaged in the China trade by sea. Whitney first went before Congress in 1845 to describe his plan to build a railroad from some site on the Great Lakes, already linked to the East Coast by canal and rails, to a port on the coast of Oregon. Whitney chose Oregon as the western end of his proposed railroad because California yet belonged to Mexico in 1845. He argued that Congress should help the project along by giving it a swath of land sixty miles wide as an inducement. Whitney was premature with his scheme, however, for a majority of the congressmen who heard him thought the idea was impractical and far too costly ever to make a profit.

Next to take up the cry for a transcontinental railroad were Southerners, who wanted the route to be a southern one because of the potential profit to their region. One spokesman for this project was James Gadsden, who in that same year of 1845, while at a railroader's convention in Memphis, Tennessee, argued for a route favorable to the South. Another to propound the same scheme was Sam Houston, hero of the Texas Revolution, former president of the Republic of Texas, and after 1845 a senator from the Lone Star State; he thought this line should run from Galveston, Texas, to San Diego, California. Such a route, said Houston, would not be too costly because of the short distance involved, yet would allow quick transportation by sea from Galveston to the East Coast of the United States.

By 1852 the many plans being advanced for a transcontinental railroad did not seem too visionary. Northerners had taken up the cry, advocating a route that began somewhere in the vicinity of Chicago and went to Puget Sound or Portland. Southerners favored New Orleans or Fort Smith or Galveston, while Midwesterners wanted a route from St. Louis. In fact, the trouble by 1852 was the many possible routes being argued as best, shortest, cheapest, and/ or easiest—but only one railroad could be built. Such a transcontinental would have to cross vast stretches of country that were almost empty of people, and a railroad made its money by carrying people, freight, and mail. Because of the distances to be overcome, the company that built this railroad would have to be given federal funds, either as a loan or as a guaranteed subsidy, in order to finance the laying of track; and after the track was laid, the company probably would operate at a loss. The federal treasury was not rich enough to pay for the building and operating of more than one transcontinental. Everyone realized this, and everyone thought one railroad would be sufficient to carry people, freight, and the mail to and from the West Coast. Thus the argument did not come on the number of transcontinentals to be built, but rather on the *one route* to be followed.

Out of this argument between Northerners and Southerners came a call for more accurate information about possible routes. Thus in 1853 Congress set aside $150,000 for the army to "ascertain the most practicable and economical route for a railroad from the Mississippi River to the Pacific Ocean." Apparently congressmen hoped that only one good route would be found, thus ending the growing sectional quarrel about where track should be laid. Jefferson Davis, who was secretary of war at this time, assigned the task to the Corps of Topographical Engineers, the map-making branch of the army. In carrying out Davis's orders, the members of the corps surveyed all possible routes with their usual competence. Lieutenant Amiel W. Whipple, late of the boundary survey, was in

85

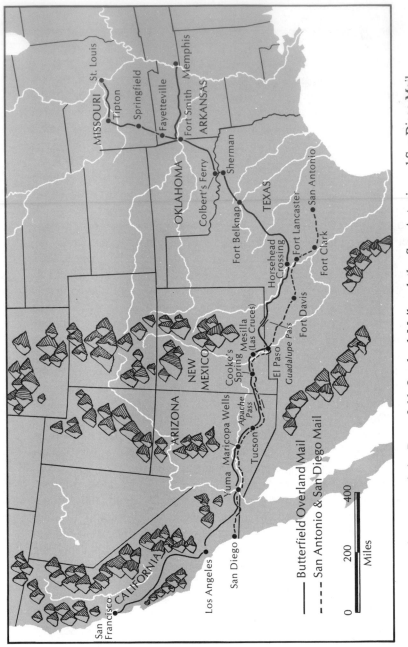

4. The routes of the Butterfield Overland Mail and the San Antonio and San Diego Mail.

charge of what became known as the thirty-fifth parallel survey, which followed Marcy's Road from Fort Smith, Arkansas, to Santa Fe and on to Los Angeles. The southernmost route surveyed was along the 32nd parallel; this was conducted under the leadership of Lieutenants John G. Parke and George Stoneman. The thirty-second parallel survey was made in 1854, after the Gadsden Purchase was concluded, and it was unique in that it was the only one of the four routes surveyed from west to east. Parke and Stoneman began their work at San Diego, entered Arizona at Yuma Crossing, went up the Gila to the Pima villages, turned up the Santa Cruz River to Tucson, and proceeded east along Cooke's Wagon Road to El Paso; from there they journeyed to the vicinity of present-day Fort Worth and Dallas and then on to Shreveport and New Orleans.

The reports turned in by the officers of the Corps of Topographical Engineers showed that there was not one good route but rather four of them, each with its individual merits and demerits: one near the Canadian border that terminated at Puget Sound, a second through the central part of the country to San Francisco, a third along the thirty-fifth parallel to Los Angeles, and a fourth along the thirty-second parallel to San Diego. All the reports were published by the Government Printing Office in ten handsome volumes which bulged with facts about the geography, geology, botany, zoology, and climate of the West; and they were illustrated with numerous excellent drawings.[1]

Moreover, at approximately the same time the Texas Western Railway Company, chartered by the state of Texas, was surveying the thirty-second parallel route. This company hired Andrew B. Gray to make its survey, which he did in 1854, meeting Lieutenant Parke en route. His report also was published,[2] although the firm that commissioned it did little else but sell stock.

All these reports left Congress deadlocked between the sectional interests of North and South and Midwest. As the year 1856 dawned, Congress had voted no funds for a transcontinental railroad, and no private firm could undertake such a gigantic scheme without help—which meant that Californians would still have to depend on ships to carry their mail. Some residents of the Pacific

87

state were so unhappy that there was occasional talk of separating the Far West from the United States and establishing a separate nation; those arguing this point of view could say that the federal government was neglecting their need for transportation and communication. Some 75,000 Californians that year signed a petition to Congress asking for a daily mail service by an overland route; interestingly, this petition called for the road to be through South Pass, which meant that the petition came mainly from northern California, where the residents wanted a route that ran almost due east to St. Louis.

Such talk and the many petitions finally spurred Congress to subsidize a transcontinental mail service by stagecoach until agreement could be reached on the transcontinental railroad. On March 3, 1857, came an act providing for carrying the mail between the Mississippi River and the Pacific Coast. In passing this act, congressmen avoided the sectional quarrel by providing that the postmaster-general would set the route. An agreement to be made by the postmaster-general with the contractor would cover a period of six years and would provide a subsidy of $300,000 annually for a twice-monthly service, $450,000 for weekly service, and $600,000 for a semi-weekly service; in each case the service was to run simultaneously both ways. The line was to run "from such point of the Mississippi River as the contractors may select, to San Francisco." Further, this service was to be performed with "good four-horse coaches or spring wagons suitable for the conveyance of passengers, as well as the safety and security of the mails." And the distance each way had to be traveled in twenty-five days or less, "the service to commence within twelve months after the signing of the contract."

The Post Office Department first advertised for bids on this contract on April 20, 1857. Most knowledgeable observers expected James Birch to get the contract. Birch, born in Rhode Island in 1827, had entered the staging business while still in his teens, then had emigrated to California in 1849, where in September he began operating stages; eventually he organized the California Stage Company which did business in northern California.

The fortune he made in this enterprise, along with the knowledge which he gained, made him seem the logical choice to organize the overland service as authorized by Congress in 1857. Moreover, he was well known in Washington, for between 1849 and 1856 he had journeyed several times to the nation's capital to consult with Congress about California's roads; in the process he had made powerful and influential friends who were expected to help him win the contract. In 1857 he was living in Massachusetts, where he had constructed a large home, from which he was in constant communication with the top men in Washington about the proposed transcontinental stage line.

The belief that Birch would get the major contract was strengthened on June 22, 1857, when the ex-California stager received a contract from the postmaster-general which called for establishing a mail route from "San Diego, via El Paso, to San Antonio, Texas." This contract was awarded under the Postal Route Bill passed by Congress on August 18, 1856; this provided a subsidy of $149,800 per year for a semi-monthly mail service, the agreement to run for four years. When Birch subsequently lost the major contract to carry the mail from the Mississippi River to San Francisco, he could console himself that his was actually a more valuable agreement than the one calling for a $600,000-per-year subsidy. The distance from San Antonio to San Diego was only 1475 miles; semi-monthly service would require only 70,000 miles of travel per year—or, to put it another way, his subsidy came to more than two dollars per mile traveled. The other route, as finally contracted, was 2800 miles in length and the service twice-weekly; it required more than 600,000 miles of travel annually but with a subsidy of only $600,000—or slightly less than one dollar per mile.

Moreover, Birch knew that his San Antonio to San Diego line would cause him little difficulty. The road was well marked and well traveled all the way, and by contract he had thirty days to make the run each way. This meant that his coaches had to make only about fifty miles per day, and this, in turn, meant that he needed only fifteen relay stations; already there were eight army posts along his route which he could use as relay stations, leaving

89

only seven new ones to be constructed. Nor would the volume of mail he had to carry be extensive. Between San Antonio and San Diego there were only two real towns: El Paso, a Mexican village in the state of Chihuahua, and Tucson, which had few people in it who could read and write English. These same facts which consoled Birch caused one newspaperman in northern California to complain that the San Diego and San Antonio Mail ran "from no place through nothing to nowhere." The Sacramento *Union* called the line a mystery and declared it to be of as much benefit to California as would be a line running from San Antonio to Guaymas, Mexico.

The contract Birch signed on June 22 called for service to begin almost immediately. Quickly he hired Isaiah Woods of New York—Major Woods he was called—and sent him by ship to Galveston; going with him on this ship were eleven new stage coaches from Abbott and Downing's factory in Concord, New Hampshire. Woods, who earlier had been associated with the Adams Express Company of San Francisco, arrived at San Antonio and began purchasing only mules to pull the coaches; he knew that mules had more strength than horses, which made the hybrid animal superior at moving the coaches through desert country. Under Woods's able direction, the first sack of mail went west from San Antonio on July 9, but by pack mule inasmuch as the way stations had not yet been built. This practice of occasionally moving the mail by mule soon led local wits to call the San Antonio and San Diego line the "Jackass Mail."

Woods's arrival at San Diego with the first sack of mail in just eleven days caused wild celebrations in the sleeply little California town. Then, his hiring of men and buying of mules completed, Woods had the stage coaches moving. The second movement of mail from San Antonio departed on July 24 by a coach driven by the celebrated old Texas Ranger William "Big Foot" Wallace.[3] Its arrival at San Diego did not lead to wild celebrating, for it arrived after a journey of thirty-eight days. Thereafter the run began at each end of the line at 6:00 a.m. on the ninth and twenty-fourth of each month. The fare one way was two hundred dollars and in-

90

cluded all meals and a baggage allowance of thirty pounds. Excess baggage was carried at a dollar per pound.

The passengers who traveled overland by the San Antonio and San Diego Mail little cared that for much of this distance they were traveling on the road pioneered by Philip St. George Cooke and the men of the Mormon Battalion. Rather they complained of the difficulties encountered. According to the printed schedule of the company, there were eighty-seven way stations; but only three of them were substantial (at San Antonio, El Paso, and San Diego), the rest being little more than brush-and-mud hovels. Yet on this route, travel was by daylight only, and at night the paying customers slept in those huts. Moreover, across the most severe portion of the journey, the desert of southern California, no stages rolled. This was the portion where travel was on muleback. In addition the food was not always edible. But the line was operating.

To get the mail moving so quickly, Woods had borrowed heavily against Birch's credit. Birch himself had departed the East Coast by ship for California, arriving in San Francisco on August 7, 1857. His business completed, he left that city on August 20 aboard the *Central America,* a ship bound for New York. On September 12 that steamer was lost in the Atlantic in a storm, Birch going down with the ship. The news of his death caused creditors of the new stage line to demand payment, and Woods would have been unable to keep the firm operating but for loans from Simeon Hart of El Paso. Birch's widow fired him in January 1858, whereupon Woods journeyed to Washington; there he persuaded the postmaster-general to transfer Birch's contract to George H. Giddings, who already was operating a mail route from San Antonio to Santa Fe, New Mexico. Giddings, this new contract in hand, joined with R. E. Doyle to form the firm of Giddings & Doyle; they operated the San Antonio and San Diego Mail Line, Isaiah Woods working as superintendent of the company.[4]

Giddings & Doyle worried only about the mail on this line, not about the passengers, but they did get the mail through in thirty days or less. Then on October 29, 1858, the postmaster-general revoked their contract to carry the mail from El Paso to Fort Yuma, for service to this area was being performed by the company given the contract to carry mail from the Mississippi River to San Francisco. Thereafter the firm of Giddings & Doyle carried the mail only from San Antonio to El Paso and from Fort Yuma to San Diego; the trip was increased to once a week instead of twice monthly, and their compensation was increased to $196,000. In the year and a quarter that this company operated as a prime carrier of transcontinental mail and people, it carried fewer than one hundred passengers across the Southwest, and its postal receipts totaled only $601.00.[5] Whatever its shortcomings and its economic failings, however, the San Antonio and San Diego Mail was the first transcontinental form of transportation moving both people and mail.

The unexpected winner of the bidding to secure the major overland mail contract, the one voted by Congress on March 3, 1857, and carrying a $600,000 subsidy, was John Butterfield and a group of business associates (which included, among others, William G. Fargo). Butterfield submitted three proposals: a semiweekly service from St. Louis to San Francisco at $585,000 annually; a twice-weekly service from Memphis to San Francisco at $595,000 annually; or a twice-weekly service from both St. Louis and Memphis to San Francisco at $600,000 annually. The emphasis on Memphis in two of these three proposals made better sense politically than geographically for the postmaster-general, Aaron Brown, was from Tennessee. Apparently Butterfield and his associates anticipated using a central route, but Brown insisted on the use of Marcy's Road and the Gila Trail; the point of convergence from St. Louis and Memphis was to be Fort Smith, Arkansas, while west of Fort Yuma the route wound northwestward to Los Angeles and then north to San Francisco. According to the term of the contract, signed on September 16, 1857, the firm was to begin operating within one year.

When the public announcement of the awarding of the contract to John Butterfield was made, northern and eastern newspapers were bitter in their denunciation. Inasmuch as Butterfield was a known friend of President James Buchanan, there were numerous protests in editorials about a political "deal" between

92

John Butterfield, founder of the Overland express.
From Harper's Monthly.

Butterfield and his friends in Washington. Actually, however, these angry denunciations were motivated more by the geography of the route, which was southern, than by politics. The New York *Herald,* which consistently had shown the greatest amount of knowledge about mail contracts in its columns, pointed out on September 16, 1858, the day service began on this line, that "The schemes of speculating contractors and land jobbers, the jealousies of various sections of the union, and clashing views of the railway companies and the machinations of politicians, all had to be met, conciliated or overthrown, and to the credit of the administration, be it said, a steady, straightforward course has been pursued. . . ."

Friends of John Butterfield were appalled when they learned of the contract he had signed calling for him to begin operating this line within one year. However, Butterfield had long experience in the staging business, and knew what he was doing. Born in New York in 1801, he had received little formal education; instead, like Birch, he had gone into staging, becoming a driver while still in his early teens. Through hard work and ability he had risen to owner-ship of several lines in New York, and in 1850 he had been one of the founders of the American Express Company. His prominence was such that by 1857 he was a personal friend of the president and of many of the most influential men of the day. Thus he signed the contract with the postmaster-general in the knowledge that he had adequate financial backing; Butterfield and Company was owned by the presidents of the major express companies in the United States: Adams; Wells, Fargo; National; and American. It was a joint stock company capitalized at $2,000,000. And it had strong political backing, for it guaranteed what Postmaster-General Brown and most Southerners wanted: a southern transcontinental route. Seemingly, then, the South had won the contest over the transcontinental, for it was widely assumed that the road pioneered by the stage line would be the route followed by the railroad whenever it was built.

Critics of the route chosen pointed out that a route running directly west from St. Louis to San Francisco would be hundreds of miles shorter and thus faster. The New York *Herald* of September

16, 1858, quoted one hostile newspaper to the effect that the government's desire to please Southerners would not "lower a mountain range or water arid plains, or make a wagon road along the face of cliffs where a mule can scarcely keep his feet. Politics are one thing and geography quite another." Postmaster-General Brown was a Southerner, and he did require Butterfield to choose a southern route, but the road established for this mail contract did prove a blessing for the new staging company; it gave them a road almost free of snow, one that could be kept open all year round and not just in the summer months.

Butterfield, after signing the contract, began working with a vigor that defied his fifty-six years. His first necessity was men; mainly he hired old and experienced frontiersmen to work for his company, men friendly with the various Indian tribes that would be encountered along the right-of-way. Then, using the most capable men from the five express companies headed by himself and his associates, he began laying out the road to be followed and erecting way-stations along the line. He decided to use the railroad building west from St. Louis to Tipton, Missouri, on the first part of the haul; between Tipton and Fort Smith, as well as Memphis and Fort Smith, he used existing roads. From Fort Smith west to California he used Marcy's Road and the Gila Trail, while inside California he again used existing roads. This gave him a route of generally hard surface and gentle grades, even over the continental divide. The route was divided into eastern and western divisions, with El Paso the dividing point; then these were subdivided into five minor divisions in the East and four in the West. Each of these minor divisions was under the direction of a superintendent. And it was these men on whom Butterfield relied to keep his stages rolling.

Where possible, the experts sent by Butterfield did not build way-stations. Rather they hired farmers to board the company's horses, and the farmhouses would serve for feeding the passengers. Across the remote stretches of the Southwest, however, there were no farmers, and in this area new way-stations did have to be built; these were constructed of adobe or of sod, while the road-building along these stretches consisted of cutting a path down

95

steep embankments at places where the rivers could be forded. Where the rivers could not be forded, Butterfield ordered ferries established rather than trying to build bridges. And when one obstacle or another could not be overcome, he simply had the road run around it. Butterfield left little of this to chance or to underlings; he personally inspected most of the route.

Beyond employees, route, and way-stations, Butterfield also had to purchase the animals and rolling stock for his line. These totaled more than a thousand horses and some seven hundred mules, eight hundred sets of harness, and about two hundred and fifty stagecoaches and spring wagons. His coaches came from three suppliers, the best known of which was Abbott and Downing of Concord, New Hampshire. This was the full-bodied stage coach so familiar in paintings of the West: a 3000-pound vehicle capable of seating nine passengers inside and as many as could pile on top; it had a capacity of 4000 pounds and cost $1400. On the inside these coaches were lined with russet leather, with cushions and even curtains of the same material. Outside some were painted red and others green. Across the top panel on each coach was lettered the title Overland Mail Company.

The wheels on these vehicles were of wood, but around each was an iron tire sufficiently broad to prevent the vehicle from sinking into the sand. Moreover, these were set five feet, two inches, apart so that the vehicle was extremely difficult to tip over. Despite the uneven terrain over which these coaches rolled, they did not have springs; rather the bodies, which were reinforced with iron, were set so that they rocked on leather straps, called thoroughbraces, which were stitched three and one-half inches wide.

These huge concords rolled at each end of the line—in Missouri, Arkansas, and California—while the rough middle portion was served by a Butterfield innovation, the "celerity" wagon. This vehicle had smaller wheels than the regular stagecoach; the body of the wagon was similar to a regular stage, but its top was a frame covered only with leather or heavy duck. Windows and doors likewise were of leather or duck, although they could be rolled up in fair, warm weather. The three seats inside were specially con-

Left.
Travelers on the Overland Mail
eating at a stage stop.
From Harper's Weekly.

Below.
A Butterfield Overland Mail coach.
Courtesy Arizona Historical Society.

structed so that their backs could be let down to lay flat and thus be made into one large bed at night for the passengers. One pilgrim who made this trip remarked of this practice that this bed was "capable of accommodating from four to ten people, according to their size and how they lie."

The tempo of Butterfield's preparations increased early in September 1858, for by the terms of his contract the first stage had to roll by September 16 that year. He and his eight hundred employees worked feverishly to stockpile hay, grain, and other supplies, along with food, at each of the nearly two hundred way-stations, just as arrangements had to be made for regular deliveries to each of them after the coaches began rolling. And drivers set out to familiarize themselves with their 60-mile stretches of the road, for to make the necessary 25-mile daily run the coaches had to roll both day and night. Therefore each driver had to know his 60-mile stretch extremely well. Conductors, who would ride beside the drivers, made a 120-mile route, and it was they who had absolute charge of the coaches.

The passenger who chose to make this ride paid two hundred dollars to ride westbound from St. Louis or Memphis to San Francisco. Those eastbound were charged only half that much as an encouragement to keep the coaches full in both directions; in 1858 there were few people leaving California. For shorter distances in either direction the fare was ten cents per mile. Each passenger was allowed to carry forty pounds of baggage free of charge; additional baggage went at one dollar per pound. And each passenger had to carry his own food or else purchase what he needed at the way-stations. The schedules called for each coach to make two meal stops a day; the price of these meals varied from forty cents to a dollar each. Some passengers later wrote that the fare was poor, but William Tallack commented, "The fare though rough, is better than could be expected so far from civilized districts, and consists of bread, tea, and fried steaks of bacon, venison, antelope, or mule flesh—the latter tough enough. Milk, butter, and vegetables can only be met with towards the two ends of the route—that is, in California and at the 'stations' in the settled parts of the western

98

Mississippi valley."[6] However, the regular fare all too often was jerked beef, beans, cornbread, and black coffee; another item found more frequently than the passengers liked was a stew referred to as "slumgullion," while mesquite beans sometimes were offered to those of large appetite.

In addition to paying for passage and food, all customers were expected to help fight troublesome Indians, to push when the stage became stuck in mud or snow or at river crossings, and to give all aid in any emergency. At the way-stations these pilgrims had a ten-minute rest stop, and the stations ranged from nine to sixty miles apart; while the passengers frantically sought a comfort station, the drivers changed horses and picked up or delivered sacks of mail. To be certain that horses were ready to be hitched, each driver carried with him a bugle which he sounded a couple of miles away from the station; this warned the station-keeper to get a relay of animals ready. The stages had to travel at an average speed of 5 miles an hour and cover 120 miles a day, 2800 miles in 25 days or less, and everyone, driver and passenger alike, was aware of John Butterfield's admonition to his employees: "Remember, boys, nothing on God's earth must stop the United States mail."

The first stage to run on the Butterfield Overland Mail departed from San Francisco on September 15, 1858, and did so with little fanfare. A newspaper in the city, the *Daily Alta California,* noted in its story that day that the coach left at one in the morning, carrying among its passengers a postal inspector named Bailey, who would be the only man to ride the entire distance to St. Louis. Bailey afterward wrote the postmaster-general that, in his opinion, the new line had met all the terms of its contract with the federal government. It had made the run to St. Louis in 23 days, 23 hours, and 30 minutes.

The westbound ride on the Overland Mail actually began as a train ride from St. Louis, for rails had been laid westward for 160 miles to Tipton, Missouri—a town that had come into being only months before with the arrival of the railroad at that point. The first coach departed on the morning of September 16 at 8:00 a.m. On board was the one passenger who had bought a through ticket to San Francisco, a twenty-three-year-old reporter for the New York *Herald,* Waterman L. Ormsby. Going with him on the first part of the journey was Butterfield himself. They arrived at Tipton that evening at six o'clock and changed to a waiting stagecoach in just nine moments.

At Fort Smith there was high excitement in the town at the arrival of the first Butterfield coach, as there would be in most western cities. Residents of big towns such as San Francisco and St. Louis might hardly notice the departure and arrival of the coaches, but elsewhere the people were very pleased at the beginning of regular mail and passenger service to the outside world. From Fort Smith the route passed through water a later traveler would call "two hundred miles of the worst road God ever built," which was the part through the Indian Territory and northern Texas. Ormsby, before he passed through this area, expressed some fear of the Indians, but was surprised to find that Choctaws had been hired as station keepers and were excellent at their jobs. Ormsby's beliefs, which were typical of those of many whites on the frontier, contrasted sharply with reality as he described a night ride across this strip:

> The night was beautifully clear and bright, and I was tempted to stay up and enjoy it; but I had become too much fatigued with the journey to be able to withstand the demands of somnolence, and, wrapping myself up in my shawls, was soon obliviously snoring on the extended seats of the wagon. I awoke but once during the night, having been jolted into a position where my neck felt as if there was a knot in it. They had stopped at a station to change horses, and for the time not a sound could I hear. I had been dreaming of the Comanche Indians, and in the confusion of drowsiness first thought that the driver and the mail agent had been murdered, and that I, being covered up with blankets, had been missed; then I recollected that I had a pistol and thought of feeling for it; but finally I thought I would not stir, for fear the Indians would see me—when I was brought to my senses by a familiar voice saying "Git up there, old hoss," and found it was the driver hitching up a new team.[7]

100

Once in Texas, that first stage met its greatest test. This was a section where many stations had not been completed, where few animals had been stocked, and where those that had been corralled often were only half broken to the harness. Valuable time was lost as mules were chased down, harnessed, and hitched, only to buck until they had nearly kicked the wagon to pieces. At last, however, they would settle down and pull.

On across the Lone Star State they raced, always aware of the schedule and their race with it. They passed the first eastbound stage one hundred miles east of El Paso—and eight hours ahead of schedule. At last the first westbound came to Franklin, opposite El Paso, to find itself running behind time. The rate of speed across Missouri and Arkansas to Sherman, Texas, had been five and one-half miles per hour; from Sherman to Fort Chadbourne, Texas, the average was three and three-quarter miles per hour; but from Fort Chadbourne to Franklin the stage had moved at only two and two-thirds miles per hour. Ormsby understandably was glad to see the last of Texas, for west of El Paso the stations had all been completed and tame animals were waiting to be harnessed. From El Paso to Tucson, the strip which crossed the continental divide, the road proved excellent—and the speed reflected this: nine miles per hour.

At Dragoon Springs, seventy-five miles east of Tucson, Ormsby noted for his readers a real western adventure of somewhat grim tone. The Mexican employees at the station had decided to murder their American bosses, steal the company property and animals, and flee south of the border; this was a common practice in the area and one that demanded close vigilance by Americans. At Dragoon Springs the Mexicans had waited until the Americans were asleep and then had attacked with axes, killing three of the four Americans immediately. The fourth, Silas St. John, defended himself with his pistol although one of his arms had been cut off in the first onslaught. He then endured three days and four nights before the first stage from San Francisco came through; taken to the hospital at Fort Buchanan, he was recovering from his wounds, hunger, and thirst.[8]

101

Right.
The Overland stage
bringing the mail
to a small town.
From Harper's Weekly.

Below.
Passengers helping
a stage up a grade.
*From Alonso Delano,
Pen Knife Sketches (1859).*

From Tucson to Los Angeles, the harshest portion of the desert, the speed averaged only five miles per hour. There they changed to the big concord stage to follow good roads and excellent way-stations to San Francisco and made nine miles per hour over the last portion. At last came the moment the New York reporter had been waiting for, the entrance into San Francisco. Of it Ormsby wrote in his last dispatch:

> Soon we struck the pavements, and, with a whip, crack, and bound, shot through the streets to our destination, to the great consternation of everything in the way and the no little surprise of everybody. Swiftly we whirled up one street and down another, and round the corners, until finally we drew up at the stage office in front of the Plaza, our driver giving a shrill blast of his horn and a flourish of triumph for the arrival of the first overland mail in San Francisco from St. Louis. But our work was not yet done. The mails must be delivered, and in a jiffy we were at the post office door, blowing the horn, howling and shouting for somebody to come and take the overland mail. . . . It was just twenty-three days, twenty-three hours and a half from the time that John Butterfield, the president of the company, took the bags as the cars moved from St. Louis at 8 a.m. on Thursday, 16th of September, 1858.[9]

When questioned about the comforts of the trip he had just completed, however, Ormsby kindly remarked, "Had I not just come out over the route, I would be perfectly willing to go back." He chose to go home by ship.

Other passengers in the next two years were not so generous in their remarks. One said of the ride, "I know what Hell is like. I've just had twenty-four days of it." A close reading of Ormsby's account does make the ride appear a difficult one; he told of sleeping very little, food that consisted principally of beans, salt pork, and black coffee, breathing dust day after day, and the threat of Indian attack. One story often repeated about the food to be had on this trip concerned a New York pilgrim who stopped at one of the Overland stations in Texas late in 1858 to find that the meal consisted of overripe sourdough biscuits and rancid bacon; unable to eat the meal, the pilgrim pushed back his plate, his mouth turning up at the corners, and glanced at the big proprietor. The proprietor misunderstood; "All right, dammit," he growled to the New Yorker, "help yourself to the mustard."[10] Some travelers could not take so many hardships at once; occasionally one of them would go insane, jump from the stage, and disappear into the desert never to be seen again. Others, hardy types, said the trip was "an exciting adventure."

President Buchanan, when informed that the first crossing had been made successfully, immediately wired Butterfield: "I congratulate you upon the result. It is a glorious triumph for civilization and the Union. Settlements will follow the course of the road, and the East and West will be bound together by a chain of living Americans which can never be broken."

Whether a triumph for civilization or a hell to be endured, an adventure to be lived or a hardship beyond description, the Butterfield Overland Mail was a reality. It became a day-to-day part of the southwestern scene, its presence taken for granted. Butterfield and his associates were primarily concerned with meeting their twenty-five-day schedule for mail delivery; with this they wanted no interference. Thus the stockholders voted, even before the first stage rolled, that no gold or silver would be carried on company stages; this fact was widely advertised and stagecoach holdups were therefore eliminated.

A second source of possible difficulty, Butterfield knew, was Indian animosity. The federal government had promised military protection, but aid from the military remained more a promise than a reality. A few infantrymen on occasion were stationed at way-stations in western Texas but Butterfield's repeated demands in Washington for more soldiers and forts along the route were to no avail.

To forestall any difficulty, Butterfield therefore warned his employees to have nothing to do with the Indians. For a time he even ordered his workers not to carry weapons, but that rule soon was retracted, and arms and ammunition were provided at all sta-

104

Indians attacking the Butterfield Overland coach on the plains.
From Harper's Weekly.

tions in the Indian country. The Indians contented themselves primarily with taking company livestock at way-stations in Arizona, New Mexico, and western Texas, and there even was an occasional attack on one of these way-stations; however, these were repulsed.

Only on one occasion was a Butterfield stage actually halted by Indian attack—and that was the result of white stupidity rather than Indian greed. On this occasion John Ward, a rancher and beef contractor living in the Sonoita Valley, became drunk and beat his wife and stepson until the boy ran away. Ward thereupon reported to the commander at nearby Fort Buchanan that Cochise, chief of the Chiricahua Apaches, had stolen his stepson and some cattle. Lieutenant George N. Bascom and fifty-four soldiers of the 7th Infantry were sent to recover the boy and the cattle from Cochise. Bascom arrived in the vicinity of the Butterfield station at Apache Pass in southeastern Arizona on February 3 and encamped three-quarters of a mile to the east. The next day Cochise came into the camp along with seven other Apaches, mostly his relatives. Bascom demanded the return of the boy and the cattle. When Cochise replied that he did not have them, a fracas ensued in which one Indian was killed and six captured. Cochise escaped to rally his warriors and attack.

That evening a wagon train entered Apache Pass. The Indians attacked, captured two Americans, and tied the eight Mexican teamsters to the wheels and burned them. The next day, February 5, the westbound Butterfield stage came to the station, changed horses, and passed through the west end of the pass; there the driver found dry grass piled in heaps across the road, but cleared it and continued toward Tucson after passing the unfortunate wagon train. Halfway to the next station, the eastbound stage was encountered—and warned; but the nine passengers were heavily armed and decided to continue. Among them was A. B. Culver, brother of the station-keeper at Apache Pass, who was conductor on the stage, and a division superintendent inspecting the line.

As this eastbound stage entered the pass, shots rang out from ambush and the two lead mules fell dead. The passengers returned the fire, while the superintendent and Culver cut the traces of the

106

lead mules; Culver then replaced the wounded driver and drove the stage on to the station, where all spent the night. The next morning, C. W. Culver, the station agent, and the driver, J. F. Wallace, along with a helper named Welch went out under a flag of truce to talk with the Indians. The Apaches were in no mood for talk, however, nor did they respect the flag of truce. Instead they rushed the three, taking Wallace a prisoner; Welch was killed trying to run, but Culver, although wounded, made it back to the station. Those remaining inside did not try to take the stage on to the east. Rather they forted up and waited for the soldiers to clear the pass.

Cochise offered to trade his three prisoners—two from the wagon train and the stage driver, Wallace—for the six Apache captives. Lieutenant Bascom refused and sent couriers to Fort Buchanan for aid. On February 10 seventy more soldiers arrived. As they scouted in the vicinity they found the bodies of the three American prisoners mutilated beyond individual recognition. The six Apache prisoners thereupon were hanged to trees near the graves of the American victims.[11] From that time until the Civil War, when the Overland Mail ran stages by the southern route, they went heavily armed.

However successful Butterfield was, his route did not please northern Californians. They wanted a line that ran directly west from St. Louis to Salt Lake City to Sacramento and San Francisco. In support of this, they argued that the run over this northern route could be made in several days less time. Butterfield agreed with their statement as it related to the summer months, but said that during the winter the northern route would be closed by snow. The northern Californians insisted such was not the case, that the northern route could be kept open year round, but Butterfield continued to follow in the footsteps of Cooke and the Mormon Battalion, insisting that this was the best and most usable route to the Pacific. His little stage stations were islands of safety in a sea of Indians, and at these American settlers huddled for protection in between their chores to keep the stages moving along.

Yet the Butterfield, with its high cost of moving the mail, could not carry freight at a reasonable cost. When it first began

107

operating, the Overland carried only letters; later it would transport newspapers and small packages. However, the goods that Southwesterners wanted and needed were bulky and were ordered in quantity. Thus they would have to come from the East in freight wagons, not stagecoaches, and at a much slower pace.

5

Freighting

On May 26, 1856, at the time when the debate was continuing over which route for a transcontinental railroad would be best, Senator John B. Weller of California arose to address his colleagues in Washington. His subject was not railroads or even a stage line to carry the mail, but rather the need of his state for good wagon roads. First he presented to the presiding officer of the Senate two heavy volumes bound in hand-tooled leather, books which he noted contained a petition signed by 75,000 Californians—the most on any petition ever presented to the Senate.

Weller then read the document to his fellow senators. It began by noting that his state numbered 500,000 residents, that through their work these citizens had developed valuable mines, ranches, and farms and that the state needed additional people to keep moving forward. For settlers to reach California, as well as to be supplied with mail and necessary supplies, they needed—desperately needed—a wagon road from the Mississippi Valley to the West Coast. "The best portion of our present population arrived here by passage across the Plains," Weller stated, and he asked that the passage of those to follow be made easier. For such a road to be usable, he wanted bridges built, ferries started on the larger streams, water holes dug, and military posts constructed to provide protection. Without these things being done, said Weller, California would remain "a distant colony." All of this could be done constitutionally, he argued, for such a road would be through federal territories, not states.

Weller reflected the Westerner's anti-intellectual attitude when he went on to state his desire that this job of road building be given to mail contractors:

They are the best road makers in the world. They do not go out, as do the topographical engineers, with barometers and other instruments, to determine the altitude of mountains; nor do they care about the botany, mineralogy or geology of the country; they take no other instruments than the ax, the shovel, the spade, and the pick-ax. Their only object is to locate a good road.

Once such a road was opened, said he, "we have no objection to parties to examine the geology and mineralogy of the country." He concluded by announcing his intention to introduce three road construction bills: one from Fort Ridgely, Minnesota, to South Pass at a cost of $50,000; a second from Missouri through Salt Lake to the Carson Valley of California at a cost of $300,000; and a third from El Paso to Fort Yuma at a cost of $200,000. Moreover, he was going to include a provision that these projects be administered by the department of the interior rather than the war department so the construction could be done by civilians, whom Weller said were "practical men."[1]

In this quest for federal funding for wagon roads to California, Weller shortly was joined by Senator Thomas J. Rusk of Texas. Rusk was interested in the project because he wanted the eastern end of one of these roads in his home state of Texas. His solution: a national wagon road to begin at the end of the Military Road from San Antonio to El Paso; this, then, would run from El Paso to Mesilla, New Mexico, to Tucson, to the Gila River, and finally to Fort Yuma, joining there with an existing road from Fort Yuma to San Diego. Rusk noted that the road he was proposing would be the cheapest of all possible routes to California and that it could be built quickly.

During the debate in the Senate, Weller's bills were referred to the Military Affairs Committee, and within a month passed that house of Congress as a military road. However, the measure providing for an El Paso-Fort Yuma road failed to pass the Republican-dominated House of Representatives because of sectional hatreds; Northerners did not want to vote money that would be expended by Secretary of War Jefferson Davis. However, in the next

110

session of Congress the bill passed the House; one of its provisions was an appropriation of $200,000 to construct the El Paso-Fort Yuma road, but the secretary of the interior—and civilians—were to supervise the construction. On February 14 the Senate approved the measure, and three days later out-going President Franklin Pierce signed it.[2]

Named road superintendent for the construction of this southern route was James B. Leach, who thought the work could proceed so rapidly that the road would be open to immigrants in 1858. His instructions from the secretary of the interior were to undertake no heavy grading or bridging but to lay out a road over which heavy wagons could pass. Moreover, he was to make provisions for collecting and preserving rainfall for drinking purposes so that travelers over the road would be assured of drinking water. Nor were they to dip so far south as had Philip St. George Cooke and the Mormons; rather they were to proceed almost due west across southern New Mexico to the San Pedro River.[3]

By late June 1857 Leach had gathered men to begin the work. Going west with him were forty wagons pulled by oxen and loaded with supplies, along with eighty mechanics and engineers and thirty-five laborers. They had 27,000 pounds of bacon, 19,225 pounds of sugar, 10,012 pounds of coffee, 234 bushels of beans, 40 barrels of vinegar, and even 2675 pounds of soap. The army furnished them with 75 rifles, 20 Colt pistols, 11,250 rifle cartridges, 3000 pistol cartridges, and 35 kegs of blasting powder. All the men and supplies were gathered at Memphis, the wagons were loaded, and all set out overland for El Paso by way of Marcy's Road from Fort Smith.

Work commenced soon after they arrived at El Paso on October 22, 1857. Leach divided the men into work parties. Some were put to drilling water wells, others to work eastward from Fort Yuma, while still others would work westward from Franklin. Brush had to be cut in the San Pedro Valley, and for this purpose sixty men, mostly Mexicans, were employed. Out of this activity there gradually grew a roadbed eighteen feet wide on the straight stretches and twenty-five feet wide on curves. Drainage culverts

111

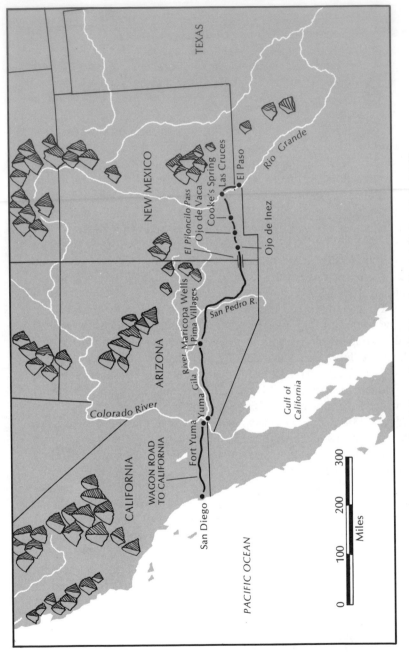

5. The Federal Wagon Road laid out by James B. Leach in 1857.

were laid, grades were reduced, and watering places made.[4] The work was completed by the end of June 1858, but Leach did not profit from it personally. Quarrels in Washington led to his being charged with misuse of government funds; he was indicted for this but never brought to trial, for the charges apparently were more political than truthful.[5]

This wagon road which Leach had engineered did open the Southwest to major freighting efforts. Goods could be sent by wagon through New Mexico and Arizona to California, or else diverted along the way into northern Mexico. Such transportation previously had been too costly. And inasmuch as this route served as an extension of the Santa Fe Trail, over which goods had moved by wagon from Missouri and the central United States since 1822, the road proved a route of commerce from the Mississippi Valley to the Far West. It became to the Southwest what the Mississippi River had been to the Midwest and what various other streams had been to the East in an earlier period; rivers had been the highways of transportation and settlement in that region, but in the arid Southwest the wagon road would be the artery of commerce. And in its own way the freight wagon was just as picturesque and as useful as flatboats and steamboats had been in the East.

In fact, the early wagons used in the Southwest had a strong similarity to boats. The prairie schooner, as it was commonly called, was an adaptation of the design commonly called Conestoga after the community in which it had originated. The Pennsylvania Dutch had excelled at building wagons, especially those in the Lancaster County town of Conestoga; there skilled craftsmen had transformed a two-wheeled cart common in Germany in the eighteenth century into a four-wheeled wagon widely known for its beauty as well as its durability. This wagon was constructed so that it was higher in front and back than in the middle, and it had a flared body wider at the top than at the bottom of the bed; some fanciers of this wagon later would claim these features were added to make the wagon float across rivers, but in reality it was so shaped to prevent the load from shifting when the wagon was going up or down hills.

113

Freight wagon crossing the Pecos River.
From John Bartlett, Personal Narrative, I.

The Conestoga weighed about four thousand pounds. Its tongue was thirteen feet long, and its rear wheels, each weighing some three hundred pounds, were five feet, four inches, in diameter. The body of the wagon was three feet, ten inches, wide, twelve feet long at the bottom, and sixteen feet long at the top. Generally the factories making these wagons painted them blue, but after some service on the frontier they were painted in various colors. When wooden bows were attached along the bed of the wagon, two sheets of canvas were stretched tightly over them to form a rain-proof cover—from which the conveyance took the name covered wagon. This kept the cargo somewhat dry and also free from dust and even hail damage.

Another type of wagon used in the Southwest and about as popular as the Conestoga was the type made by Joseph Murphy of St. Louis. Murphy built his wagons using only seasoned wood of high quality and drilling his bolt holes with a hot iron to a size slightly smaller than the bolts themselves; this use of the hot iron instead of an auger (drill), prevented the wood from cracking around the bolts. The bed of the Murphy wagon was sixteen feet long and six feet high, and the rear wheels were seven feet in diameter. By the end of the Mexican War, iron was available in sufficient quantity to provide iron axles and iron tires around the wooden wheels, but iron tires always presented a problem in the arid Southwest. The wooden part, fashioned in the humid East, would contract in the desert, and the iron rim would fall off. Teamsters therefore learned to remove their wheels at night, and perhaps even during the noon halt, to soak them in a river or a water hole.

These wagons, clumsy and ungainly by farmers' standards, would carry some 6500 pounds of freight, however, and they were built of such heavy wood that a breakdown on the trail was most unlikely. Moreover, the Murphy and Conestoga wagons were almost impossible to overload; their size made it difficult to load them with anything of sufficient weight to break the heavy wood used in their construction.

East of the Mississippi River, four- and six-horse teams had pulled the wagons, and such was the practice as the pioneers

115

Above.
The bullwhacker at work
on the plains in the 1850s.
From Harper's Weekly.

Right.
A western freighter at work.
From Harper's Weekly.

crossed this river and moved immediately west of it. But on the plains, teamsters quickly learned that the horse did not have enough strength or endurance for this task. In the western region the animals had to be fed on grass, not grain, and grass did not keep a horse's strength up as it would that of an ox or a mule. Also, horses were subject to many diseases that did not bother mules and oxen. Finally, horses were a prime target for theft by Indian raiders whereas mules were only to a lesser extent and oxen not at all. Thus a good mule came to be valued at two to three times that of a horse, and a Mexican mule was worth more than his American counterpart; interestingly, most American teamsters considered the Mexican mule to have a higher degree of intelligence than his contrary and stubborn American counterpart.

The ox, however, was far cheaper than horses or mules. He was gentle, inexpensive to feed, and almost impossible to stampede. Moreover, an ox had one other advantage: if disabled, he could be slaughtered and his meat added to the daily menu, whereas teamsters would not eat horse flesh, and they considered mule meat too tough to devour. For these reasons, oxen were used almost exclusively unless the freight needed quick delivery, in which case the wagons would be pulled by mules or horses. Some Texas teamsters so preferred oxen that when these were unavailable they turned to longhorn steers. A good pair of oxen cost about fifty dollars, and six or eight, certainly ten of them, could pull a wagon anywhere in the Southwest.

The driver of such a team was called a bullwhacker in this period. Those men who drove mules—or even horses—were known as muleskinners. On occasion these drivers would ride, but generally they walked on the left side of the animals. Finding young men willing to undertake this occupation was easy, for bullwhacking and muleskinning was considered a life of adventure and romance by most young lads on the frontier. Most of these lads thought their education was incomplete unless they had crossed the plains and desert at least once as a bullwhacker. These men did possess a certain degree of skill, but it was little beyond that which every farm boy learned as he grew up.

117

When ranked against stagecoach drivers and riverboat pilots, however, the bullwhacker ran a poor third in public estimation. Generally such a man was illiterate and profane, he drank as much as possible, and he was given to brawling. His clothes—an old hat, a ragged flannel shirt, buckskin or store-bought trousers, and brogan shoes—usually were dirty, as were his face and hands. Yet he considered himself a "duke of the road," a man of far more stature than townsmen, farmers, and especially the men who loaded and unloaded his freight. He took pride in his profession, and he showed it in the bells with which he adorned his harness and in his whip.

The bullwhacker's whip weighed about five and one-half pounds. The short handle was made of tough ash or pecan wood, and attached to it was a lash two inches in diameter and some ten feet in length. The lash was made from undressed rawhide, the tip a thong of buckskin. The weight and length of this instrument meant that to carry it all day would sap a man's strength, while to snap it occasionally would build strong arms. Actually the driver seldom struck an ox with his whip; rather he cracked it with a flourish and a jerk that produced a sound like a pistol shot. Occasionally, however, one of the oxen would require discipline, and then the tip would hit him, raising a mist of hair and blood like the cut of a bullet. These teamsters gloried in their whips and in their ability to use them, for it at once was a sign of manhood and of membership in a tough fraternity of men.

The driving of eight or ten mules or oxen was an art of sorts. In this the muleskinner or bullwhacker depended mainly on his "lead team." These animals, when rightly trained, were controlled by a single "jerk line" which extended from the bit on the left front animal back through collar rings to the teamster. This he held in one hand, his whip in the other. In order to coordinate the movements of this left lead animal with his partner, the right front lead animal, the teamster fastened a stick about the size of a broom handle between the two animals; this forced them to work together. When the teamster wanted to turn right, he signaled this to the left lead animal with a series of jerks and the vocal command "gee." A

118

Freighters in camp on the plains. *From Harper's Monthly.*

turn to the left was signaled by a steady pull on the jerk line and the vocal command "haw." And, of course, he used profanity liberally.

For this work in the 1850s, bullwhackers were paid some twenty-five to thirty dollars a month. They were given their food and there was no cost for lodging inasmuch as they slept under the stars or, in rainy weather, under their wagons. Because they slept outside they hated the weather; dust storms, snow, ice—any of these were sufficient to bring forth the strongest words at the bull-whacker's command, and they were strong indeed. In comparison with the drivers, the wagon master, who had charge of the freight wagon, was wealthy, for he received as much as one hundred dollars per month plus his meals.

The food was not the kind to please a pilgrim with a delicate stomach. For each month a wagon train was to be on the trail, a driver was allowed fifty pounds of bacon, ten pounds of coffee, fifty pounds of flour, twenty pounds of sugar, and some salt. It was expected that he would supplement this with fresh meat, such as buffalo or antelope or deer; when someone shot a wild animal, the meat was cut into strips like ropes, and these were hung over the sides of the wagons to dry; this process was known as "jerking," and the result generally was referred to as "jerky." The teamsters considered jerky to be a delicacy far superior to bacon, and thus when meat animals were sighted the wagon train generally came to a halt and hunting followed. The dead animals were butchered as fast as possible, the meat cut into strips, and then, dripping blood from the sides of their wagons, the train moved on.[6]

At San Antonio or St. Louis wagon trains readying for the trail were a colorful sight. Outside of town thousands of oxen grazed as they waited to be hitched up. In town the streets rumbled as heavy wagons already loaded were pulled into a camping ground, filled with sacks, barrels, and boxes until they totaled about six thousand pounds. Whips cracked and men sweated and cursed, while the bullwhackers sat drinking in taverns or sunned themselves in the streets, leisurely spending their wages as they waited for the lowly townsmen to ready their prairie schooners.

A mule freight train in Tucson. *Courtesy Arizona Historical Society.*

Carriages, men, horses, mules, and oxen moved about in a confused blur; oxen lowed and mules brayed; dust rose high—until at last every wagon was loaded and at the camp ground.

Then came the wagon master's cry to start the train. The teamsters cracked their whips while the air turned blue from forty, fifty, or more voices trying to outdo one another at profanity. Gradually the balky oxen would get moving, and order would emerge from chaos. The wagon master then would mount his mule, and the wagon train would move beyond the horizon. On such a drive as this, the men expected to follow a set routine. The firm of Russell, Majors and Waddell later would codify the accepted practice into a set of rules followed in their freighting operations: at daylight, drive one or two miles and then halt to allow the animals to breathe; then drive until about ten o'clock in the morning, usually another seven to ten miles, and halt to allow the oxen to graze for two hours while the men prepared and ate their breakfast; there followed another drive of seven to ten miles, another halt for grazing and a meal; finally, there was yet another drive, this one lasting until dark, at which time camp was made.[7] A typical day's drive was fourteen to eighteen miles, after which the oxen were turned out to graze under the supervision of a mounted herder known as the "cavie." Generally the men ate in groups of six to eight, taking turns at the cooking chore of preparing bread, bacon, and coffee. After the evening meal, someone would produce a deck of greasy cards, and the bullwhackers would play cards, tell tall stories, and even sing a few songs before turning in. Such would be the order of their days until they reached their final destination. There were no stops for observing the Sabbath or for holidays.

Prior to the opening of the El Paso to Fort Yuma road, the cost of bringing merchandise into the Southwest had been very high. Supplies came north from Mexico into Arizona and New Mexico aboard huge carts drawn by oxen, while in California merchandise came only by sea. The vehicle in New Mexico and Arizona was the Spanish *careta*, a big, cumbersome, and rough vehicle that was exceedingly slow. Drawn by oxen, these took six months to make the trip from central Mexico north to Santa Fe or Tucson, and their capacity was limited to some two thousand pounds of goods. This type of transportation had changed but little since Biblical days and was unsuited to the needs of a dynamic Southwest where people were demanding large quantities of goods. Yet these Mexican carts continued to roll even after the arrival of the Conestogas, their wooden wheels grinding against wooden axles with a screech that could be heard for miles. They came up the Santa Fe Trail to Kansas City, and they went down the new road from New Mexico into Arizona, just as they continued to journey southward to bring goods from central Mexico into the region.

Another change made necessary by the rapid increase of population in Arizona and along the Gila Trail was a lowering of the high cost of moving goods into the region. In 1849 the cost was astronomically high. For example, in 1849 when the army first established Fort Yuma to protect pilgrims using the Gila Trail in their quest to get to the gold fields of California, quartermaster officers contracted with teamsters to bring supplies the 180 miles from San Diego overland to the new post. Captain Rufus Ingalls, the quartermaster for Fort Yuma, later said, "From San Diego to Fort Yuma there is but one known practable [sic] wagon route, and it passes over, perhaps, the worst and most irksome desert for beasts in the world. There are more extensive deserts than this great 'American desert'; but considering the distance to be passed over, it is as hazardous and pernicious as so much of Sahara or Gobi." He also noted that in 1851 Fort Yuma had to be abandoned for a time because of "the enormous expense of furnishing supplies and the small amount furnished."[8] This cost was $500 to $800 per ton—for moving goods only 180 miles.

In the shadow of this fort on the Arizona side of the river grew the little town of Yuma, and it was a local resident of this village who demonstrated the fortune that could be made by providing transportation in the region. L. J. F. Jaeger, a native of Pennsylvania who arrived at Yuma in 1850, started a ferry across the Colorado (in addition to the one operated by the Yuma In-

Louis J. F. Jaeger, freighter and ferry operator.
Courtesy Arizona Historical Society.

dians). He charged $1 for ferrying a man across the river, $2 for a horse or mule, and $5 for a wagon. Soon he realized sufficient profit from this operation to begin the purchase of wagons and teams with which to get into the freighting business. Also, he supplied the army with hay at $60 per ton, a venture that proved highly profitable. And he grew rich from these enterprises, his wagons regularly rolling as far west as San Diego and Los Angeles and as far east as Santa Fe and El Paso. For a time he even was freighting copper ore a hundred miles from the east at the little mine called Ajo, taking it to the mouth of the Colorado River where it was put aboard ship and carried to Wales, England, for smelting—all this at a profit to the operators of the copper mine.[9]

Prior to the Civil War, the largest freighting firm in this region, as well as in the entire American West, was that of Russell, Majors and Waddell. In 1848 Alexander Majors had started this operation with six teams on the Santa Fe Trail, which meant he had a considerable amount of capital by this time. A wagon cost from $500 to $1000; the addition of oxen or mules plus harness doubled or even tripled that figure. Then in 1853 two other former Santa Fe traders, William H. Russell and William B. Waddell, took a government contract to haul goods from the lower Missouri River to Fort Riley, Kansas, and to Fort Union, New Mexico. A year later they asked Majors to join them, their express purpose to haul merchandise to army posts in the West and Southwest and to buy and sell general merchandise for purposes of transport.[10]

Alexander Majors was best known for his religious attitude against cursing, a pastime at which bullwhackers reportedly were the best in the world. Whenever a teamster asked Majors for a job, he reportedly would ask if the applicant could drive a team across the plains and back without swearing. One Irishman once answered Majors, a former Methodist minister, by saying, "Yes, I can drive a team to hell and back without swearing." Majors considered that cursing, and the man was not hired.

Russell, Majors, and Waddell rose to preeminence in 1857 when it secured the government contract to supply the army bound for Utah during the so-called Mormon War. This one contract

125

Mule freight teams used to haul ore. *Courtesy Arizona Historical Society.*

alone was valued at $500,000, and by the following year the firm had 4000 men working for it, with 3500 wagons and 40,000 oxen on the road.

A small firm by comparison, but one which would come to dominate Southwestern freighting after the Civil War ended, was one headquartered at Tucson, Arizona, and owned in part by Estevan Ochoa. Born in Chihuahua City, Mexico, in 1831, Ochoa as a lad had moved with his family to New Mexico, and there he saw at firsthand the riches being made by Santa Fe traders from Missouri. His family saw the wave of the future and sent young Estevan to Independence, Missouri, for his education—and so he could learn the English language along with Yankee business methods. Afterward he returned to New Mexico, and there he became first a Santa Fe trader, learning the freighting business the hard way: as a bullwhacker. Then, following the American conquest of New Mexico, he entered into business with Pedro Aguirre and

126

opened his own store in the little town of Mesilla. There he profited from sales to men venturing across the Gila Trail to California during the gold rush; these profits were high inasmuch as he brought his own freight and avoided that cost.

With the money he saved from these two ventures, Ochoa soon had stores in several cities in New Mexico, his own wagons hauling in the goods to stock their shelves. Eventually he grew tired of having to split his profits with Aguirre, and in 1859 he dissolved the partnership. The following year he moved westward to Tucson, a town which he correctly foresaw had a bright future, and there for the next four decades he would be one of the leading citizens. Standing only some five feet, four inches, tall, he was a quiet man, even reportedly being even tempered with oxen and mules, a quality rare among bullwhackers. By the coming of the Civil War, Ochoa had become one of Arizona's richest and best known citizens. His wagons were rolling from San Diego to Kansas City, bringing merchandise to be distributed to stores in New Mexico and Arizona.[11]

The freighter has not become as famous as the soldiers who opened the wagon road to California, as glamorous as the Forty-Niners who used it to reach the golden West, nor yet as written about as the stage-drivers who guided Concords across the desert to deliver the mail. But he was equally an instrument of civilization, for he brought the clothes these people wore, the food they ate, the seeds for the crops they planted, and the furnishings for the homes they built—and in the process made a profit. Generally, however, he is not remembered as a positive factor in the building of the region, but rather as a man noted for his ability to curse.

Yet the activities of all these men—stage-drivers, miners, bull-whackers, certainly the soldiers—were interrupted by the storm clouds of war gathering over the Republic. And the storm broke early in 1861, even involving the Gila Trail in its cloudburst of destruction and death.

6

Civil War Along the Trail

On the afternoon of July 25, 1861, approximately three hundred Union soldiers under the command of Major Isaac Lynde approached the little town of Mesilla, New Mexico. These blue-clad troops and their commander were aware that the town had been occupied that morning by Lieutenant Colonel John Robert Baylor and 258 Confederates of the Second Texas Regiment. Lynde sent Lieutenant Edward J. Brooks and Surgeon James C. McKee ahead with a flag of truce to demand an "unconditional surrender of the forces and the town!" According to one report, Baylor replied to this ultimatum, "We will fight first and surrender afterward!"[1]

And fight the Texans did. Their fire was so withering and their spirits so strong that Lynde and his federal troops soon retired from the field of battle to the safety of nearby Fort Fillmore. This skirmish, as well as the reply made to the demand for a surrender, showed the fiery character of the self-styled Confederate governor of Arizona, as well as ended the first major battle of the Civil War to take place along the Gila Trail. Its outcome meant that most of this road immediately became a part of the Confederacy—at least temporarily.

The bloody events of that day had their origin in the quarrel that had developed in the eastern United States. For years leaders of the Southern states had proclaimed their right to secede from the Union, and they even had threatened to do this on several occasions as they argued with their Northern brothers about the issue of states' rights. Then came the election of Abraham Lincoln, a sectional candidate of the sectional Republican party, and the argument moved from the abstract to the concrete. Cold reason told

Southerners that the president could not abolish slavery; only a constitutional amendment could do that. Nor could the new president do many other things so long as Southerners remained in Congress and voted against the chief executive's programs. But these Southerners did not live by cold reason, but by hot emotions, and in anger they began transforming their threat of secession into reality. On December 20, 1860, South Carolina led the way, and one by one the other Southern states followed.

In Texas, which controlled the eastern approaches to the Gila Trail, a secession convention met in Austin, the state capital, on January 26, 1861. Governor Sam Houston, the aging hero of Texas independence, who had returned from the United States Senate in 1859 to become the state's chief executive, thought secession was stupid and the Southern cause hopeless. "You may, after the sacrifice of countless thousands of treasure and hundreds of thousands of precious lives, as a bare possibility win Southern independence, if God be not against you," he told an audience in Galveston, "but I doubt it." He was right, but it would take billions of dollars and more than a million lives to prove him so.

The delegates to the Texas secession convention disagreed with their governor, however, for they lacked his foresight. On January 30, with only eight dissenting votes, they shouted through a resolution of secession. Soon afterward the people of the state voted on the issue and passed it by a margin of three to one, making Texas the seventh state to withdraw from the Union.

Not only did the delegates to the secession convention want to break the tie to the United States, but also they wanted to join the newly organizing Confederacy, and they desired to expand toward the Pacific. Actually there was little economic reason to try to take this western region. Obvious in both North and South was the fact that whichever side won the war would also win ownership of the West. New Mexico and Arizona were thinly settled; there was no large population along the Gila Trail from which to draw volunteers for battle, few farms and ranches from which to get food, no factories from which to get the goods of war, no transportation system other than wagons to be taken or destroyed.

130

There were only Indians who would be happy to see the whites killing one another.

The West did have mines, however, and from these were pouring gold and silver. Whichever side controlled the Gila Trail would own the approach to California and Nevada—and the owner of these mining areas would have a psychological advantage with foreign countries. If the South could gain control of the Southwest and of the mines, then Confederate money would be worth face value; without it, the Confederate dollar would gradually become worth less and less. Thus Texans and other Southerners wanted to capture New Mexico and Arizona first and then California and Nevada.

The delegates at that Texas secession convention were convinced that the people living in the Territory of New Mexico, which then included Arizona, would join the Southern cause happily. Therefore they appointed commissioners to invite the New Mexicans likewise to secede. One of these commissioners, Simeon Hart, on February 1, 1861, wrote a strong letter to the *Mesilla Times*, which printed the letter three weeks later. In this, Hart called on residents of what he called the Gadsden Purchase area (the southern half of present New Mexico and Arizona) to join with "those who have ever sympathized with you" against the "fanaticism of the North." Hart suggested that a secession convention be held at Mesilla on March 16 to take the region out of the Union and into the Confederate camp.

This call met an enthusiastic response along the Gila Trail in Arizona and New Mexico, for most of the settlers were Southern sympathizers. Thus the suggested convention did meet at Mesilla on March 16. The other commissioner from Texas appointed by the secession convention, Philemon T. Herbert, talked to those gathered there, but it was his law partner, W. Claude Jones, who most aroused the delegates with a speech. "Has not [the North] treated us with cold and criminal neglect," Jones thundered at them, "and has this corrupt sectional party [the Republicans] taken any steps toward our organization [as a territory separate from New Mexico]?" As he continued, he warmed to his subject, then

131

concluded with the call: ". . . The hell of abolitionism glooms to the north—the Eden of liberty, equality, and right smiles upon you from the south! Choose ye between them."[2]

And choose the delegates did, unanimously—to secede. In their resolution they condemned the Republican party, broke their ties with the Union, and asked to join the Confederacy. The senior federal army officer in New Mexico, Colonel (later General) Edward R. S. Canby,[3] did not help the situation by his response; one of his first orders was to withdraw all Union soldiers from along the Gila Trail to central New Mexico along the Rio Grande to fight off the Confederate invasion he expected to come soon. This left the people along the Gila Trail without military protection just at a time when the Apaches of the region had been given strong reason to go on the warpath in great numbers; following the tragic Bascom Affair, Cochise was devastating the area.

The Confederates wasted no time in trying to take advantage of the pro-Southern sentiment in New Mexico and Arizona. Again it was the Texas secession convention which initiated the action. On March 19, 1861, this body voted to raise a second regiment of mounted volunteers. John S. "Rip" Ford was elected the colonel to command this regiment of one thousand men, and John R. Baylor was selected to be its lieutenant colonel.

Baylor was born in Kentucky in 1822 and attended a university in Cincinnati before moving to Texas in 1840 to live near the village of LaGrange. There he farmed, and like everyone else fought the Comanches, those lordly masters of the plains whose early friendliness with the American pioneers of Texas had turned to hatred after the infamous Council House Fight at San Antonio in March 1840; during this engagement several of their chiefs had been killed.[4] And he fought the Mexicans before going into the law and public life, finally settling west of Fort Worth to ranch. Then came the Civil War and with it the offer of a commission as a lieutenant colonel of the Second Regiment of Texas Mounted Volunteers. Baylor accepted the commission, which made him a part of the regular Confederate army.

Commanding the Department of Texas for the Confederacy

132

John Robert Baylor, Confederate governor of Arizona.
Courtesy Arizona Historical Society.

Mesilla, New Mexico, in 1852. *Courtesy Library of Congress.*

was Colonel (later General) Earl Van Dorn, who ordered Rip Ford to take the major portion of the Second Regiment to the Rio Grande Valley and secure it; the remainder, four companies, were to march under Baylor's orders to take Fort Bliss at El Paso. Van Dorn reminded Baylor that Fort Bliss was only thirty-eight miles south of Fort Fillmore, New Mexico, which was garrisoned by federal troops. Baylor was to be prudent, said Van Dorn, but he was to capture the post if possible, for it controlled the Gila Trail and the gateway to the West.[5]

During the latter part of June and the first week of July, Baylor was at El Paso and securely in command of Fort Bliss; this post surrendered without a battle. Next he busied himself collecting information about conditions in southern New Mexico, especially about the Union troops at Fort Fillmore.[6] He discovered that the people in the recently acquired Gadsden strip area were strongly pro-Southern in their attitude and sympathies as he had heard they were, that in fact they had already passed a resolution asking annexation to the Confederacy. But General Canby had strengthened Fort Fillmore and had sent Major Isaac Lynde to take command and defend the region. Baylor learned of the increase in federal troops at the post and interpreted it to mean that Canby was planning an offensive move against western Texas. He determined to strike first without waiting for orders from his commander, General Van Dorn.

Moving northward, Baylor at first hoped he would catch Fort Fillmore by surprise. However, in this he failed, and therefore occupied the nearby town of Mesilla instead; marching into the little village on the morning of July 25, he and his men were greeted with "vivas and hurrahs" by the local citizens. That afternoon Major Lynde moved his federal troops up to do battle, but soon retreated ingloriously. Union casualties totaled three dead and six wounded. Baylor reported he had no losses. The following evening of July 26 the timorous Lynde set fire to the military stores at Fort Fillmore, and during the early evening hours of the twenty-seventh began marching his men northward toward the nearest federal outpost.

135

The light of dawn revealed to Baylor what had happened, and he hurriedly gathered 162 of his men to give chase. Lynde's trail was easy to follow, not only because of the dust raised by the column of Union troops but also because the road was lined with straggling Yanks who had fallen out of the line of march due to heat and exhaustion. When Baylor reached the head of the column, Lynde sounded the call to arms but only about one hundred of his men were able to respond. He therefore decided resistance was useless and surrendered unconditionally. Not a shot had been fired. "Honor did not demand the sacrifice of blood after the terrible suffering," Lynde later would write in defense of his action. The victory was a significant one for the Confederates: not only had Baylor captured an army almost twice as large as his own—and with no casualties—but also he had captured all the federal transportation equipment, arms, ammunition, commissary and quartermaster stores, and four pieces of artillery, along with $9500 in United States drafts (of which he succeeded in cashing $4500). The Union prisoners were taken back to Mesilla, where they were paroled, mainly because Baylor was unable to feed them.[7] The *Mesilla Times* headlined the story, "ARIZONA IS FREE AT LAST."[8]

As a result of Lynde's blundering, Union government and control collapsed in southern New Mexico. Other federal detachments hastily withdrew, leaving Baylor in complete command of the area. The Texan proceeded to establish a semi-military government; on August 1 he issued a proclamation stating that he had taken formal possession of the "Territory of Arizona." He declared, "The social and political condition of Arizona being little short of general anarchy, and the people being literally destitute of law, order and protection, the said Territory from the date hereof, is hereby declared temporarily organized as a military government, until such time as [the Confederate] Congress may otherwise provide."

He set the boundary of this territory at the thirty-fourth parallel on the north, stretching from Texas to the Colorado River. This proclamation declared Baylor to be the governor, the capital to be Mesilla, and all United States civil and military offices to be vacant.[9] The following day Baylor issued a list of territorial appointees, and on August 14 he wrote General Van Dorn that Arizona had a functioning provisional government. That same letter also announced his intention to move the northern boundary of his territory northward to 36° 30′ north latitude.[10] The Confederate government at Richmond, Virginia, did subsequently approve all these actions except moving the boundary northward, and Baylor was promoted in rank to colonel. Well the Southern leaders might approve, for through his actions the impetuous Texan had given them control of the eastern access to the most vital route of transportation and communication with California, the Gila Trail.

Within a week of Baylor's establishment of a Confederate Territory of Arizona, the citizens of Tucson, the only major town on the Gila Trail between Mesilla and California, held a mass meeting at which they expressed their approval. Already there had been demonstrations of Confederate sympathy at the town: on March 23 a public gathering had been held, at which Mark Aldrich, the richest man in town, presided; it had denounced the North and had asked the Confederacy to extend to Arizona "the protection necessary to the proper development and advancement of the Territory." And when news of the Southern victory at Fort Sumter had reached Tucson in mid-May, a wild celebration followed, during which a Confederate flag was presented to a volunteer company of "Arizona Rangers," an improvised military band played "Dixie's Land," and the Confederate banner was raised above Joshua Sledd's billiard saloon. The withdrawal of Union troops eastward by General Canby had further alienated Arizonans, for this left them without protection from the Apaches.

Thus, at the meeting at Tucson in August 1861, the local citizens elected Granville H. Oury their delegate to the Confederate congress. Oury, a former Texan, proceeded to Richmond where on November 22, 1861, John H. Reagan, another Texan, introduced a bill in the Confederate congress to organize a Territory of Arizona. This bill subsequently passed both houses and was signed into law by President Jefferson Davis on January 18, 1862; it was

Granville H. Oury, who represented Arizona in the Confederate congress. *Courtesy Arizona Historical Society.*

to take effect on February 14 that year. This act declared the northern boundary of the territory to be 34° north latitude, but stipulated that the Confederacy reserved the right to occupy all or any part of New Mexico north of this line. Oury at this time was seated as the territorial delegate from Arizona in the Confederate congress.[11] Soon after the passage of this bill, President Davis named Baylor the governor of Arizona; his salary was set at $1500 annually, and he was to receive an additional $500 as commissioner of Indian affairs.[12]

As governor of Arizona, Colonel Baylor had two immediate and pressing problems: what to do about the Apaches, who had virtually closed the Gila Trail in their quest for revenge following the Bascom Affair, and the threat from the north posed by General Canby and his Union troops. Of these two problems, the most serious threat to Baylor's governorship was the 2500 federal soldiers commanded by Canby and stationed some 117 miles upriver from Mesilla at Fort Craig, the nearest Union outpost. During the fall of 1861 Baylor was so concerned that these soldiers would come marching downstream that he made plans to abandon Mesilla and fall back into western Texas. Robert P. Kelley, the editor of the *Mesilla Times* and a rabid Southern patriot, published a strong editorial criticizing Baylor for these preparations; in his issue of December 12, 1861, Kelley said the Texan's preparations for flight were based more on fear than on military necessity. Baylor did not like being called a coward by implication, and he demanded a public apology from Kelley. When this was not forthcoming, the two men fought a duel in the streets of Mesilla using knives as weapons. Baylor emerged the victor, the editor dying on January 1, 1862, from the wounds he received.[13] Despite Kelley's editorials about Baylor's lack of courage, General Canby remained at Fort Craig, and thus the Confederate governor could turn his attention to the Apache menace along the Gila Trail.

Baylor's answer to Cochise's raids was to raise a group of volunteers from within Arizona and western Texas whom he designated the Arizona Guards and the Arizona Rangers. The latter group was mustered into the service under the command of Captain George M. Frazer, and numbered approximately thirty-five men. The Guards were led by Captain Thomas Helm and consisted of some thirty troops.[14] These men Baylor ordered to reopen the road between Mesilla and Tucson, especially to rout the natives from Apache Pass. Despite these efforts, however, the situation deteriorated. By the spring of 1862 the Indians commanded almost every acre of land in Confederate Arizona; only in Tucson and Mesilla where there was safety in numbers could whites sleep safely at night.

Governor Baylor drew on his past experience in Texas in hunting for a solution to this problem. "The only good Indian is a dead Indian"—so ran the frontier maxim, a philosophy to which the Confederate governor subscribed wholeheartedly. He believed a white man was justified in taking any measure in order to accomplish this transformation. Therefore on March 20, 1862, from his home in Mesilla he wrote Captain Helm of the Arizona Guards at Tucson:

> I learn from Lieut. J. J. Jackson that the Indians have been in to your post for the purpose of making a treaty. The Congress of the Confederate States has passed a law declaring extermination to all hostile Indians. You will therefore use all means to persuade the Apaches or any tribe to come in for the purpose of making peace, and when you get them together kill all the grown Indians and take the children prisoners and sell them [as slaves] to defray the expense of killing the Indians. Buy whisky and such other goods as may be necessary for the Indians and I will order vouchers given to cover the amount expended. Leave nothing undone to insure success, and have a sufficient number of men around to allow no Indians to escape.[15]

Before this plan could be put into effect, however, the situation in Confederate Arizona changed drastically, the result of Southern attempts to conquer all of New Mexico. During the final months of 1861, while Baylor was worrying about Kelley's insults to his honor and about the Indian problem, another Confederate expedition had entered the region. This was one commanded by Henry Hopkins Sibley. A Virginian by birth, Sibley had been a major in the United States army in 1861 when the war started, but he was bitter at his failure to be promoted to a higher rank. Although at one time he apparently had been a competent soldier—and he was the inventor of the Sibley tent and the Sibley stove, which would be widely used by the United States army—he was a heavy drinker by May 13, 1861, when he resigned his commission and left New Mexico, where he had been serving. Arriving at the Confederate capital, he told President Jefferson Davis of the ease with which he believed New Mexico would fall into Southern hands. Davis liked what Sibley said, and on July 8 he commissioned Sibley a brigadier general in the Southern army with orders to raise a brigade of cavalry in Texas, march these men to New Mexico, conquer the territory, and become its governor.[16]

With this commission in hand, Sibley went to San Antonio and began to recruit. He used the newspapers to spread the news of his enterprise, and soon men began to flock to his standard to form three regiments of Texas Volunteer Cavalry. Most of these troops were young, their ages ranging from seventeen to twenty-one. All were well mounted and clothed, but they were poorly armed because weapons were difficult to secure and because they had to provide their own; thus there was a wide diversity of firearms. Wrote one participant: ". . . We were armed with squirrel-guns, sportsman's-guns, shotguns, both single and double barrels, in fact, guns of all sorts, even down to guns in the shape of cannons called 'Mountain Howitzers.' " In addition, almost all of them carried twenty-inch Bowie knives made by hometown blacksmiths.[17]

This "Army of New Mexico," as it was styled, departed from San Antonio late in October and early in November 1861, arriving at El Paso in mid-December. There Sibley assumed command of all Confederate forces in the West, including those of Baylor. And on December 20 he issued a proclamation to the people of New Mexico in which he listed the many benefits of Confederate rule and protection; moreover, he invited one and all—Union soldiers as well as civilians—to join with him and the southern cause. On

141

that same date he promulgated General Orders No. 12 which stated that his prior proclamation was not "intended to abrogate or supersede the powers of Col. John R. Baylor, as civil and military governor of Arizona."[18] From El Paso he marched on north to Mesilla. There he rested briefly while ordering two hundred men westward to Tucson before moving on up the Rio Grande to fight Canby at Fort Craig.

These two hundred men, called the "Arizona Volunteers," were commanded by Captain Sherrod Hunter. They arrived in Tucson on February 28 to be greeted by an enthusiastic population. Union sympathizers either remained silent, slipped away to California, or else saw their property confiscated and themselves ordered out of town. Hunter and his men did make a few attempts to fight the Apaches, but mainly their drive was to the west, to California, which they hoped might come into Southern hands. One detachment of his men got as far west on the Gila Trail as the Pima Indian villages on the Gila River; there, to their surprise, they found supplies being stockpiled for a Union force coming from California.

At the outbreak of the war, however, California was anything but certain for the Union column, but with one peculiar twist: it likewise was not certain for the Southern camp. In fact, the governor of California, former boundary commissioner and former United States senator, John B. Weller declared early in 1861 that his state should not choose between the two sides but should establish on the Pacific shore "a mighty republic, which may in the end prove the greatest of all." That call did not generate high enthusiasm and died shortly.

The northern part of the state soon began to manifest a strong Union sentiment, but in the southern half of the state most of the people seemed to favor the South. In Los Angeles and San Diego the newspaper editorials, along with speeches by politicians, called for secession and joining the Confederacy. Finally General George Wright, who commanded the troops in the state, refused to allow several pro-Southern newspapers to be carried by the United States mail, and he declared that he would hang traitors. That halted the

General James H. Carleton, commander of the California Volunteers in the Civil War. *Courtesy Arizona Historical Society.*

most outspoken calls for secession, but California did remain so doubtful to the Union that the draft laws were never applied there and few who enlisted in the state were sent east to fight. The most famous unit from the state to see service in the war was the California Column commanded by Colonel (later General) James Henry Carleton, a New Englander with political and financial ambitions. When Carleton learned of the Confederate invasion of New Mexico and Arizona, he prepared his two thousand men for marching, and he sent agents ahead to stockpile supplies for them; these were the men found by Sherrod Hunter's troops at the Pima villages on the Gila River.

One of Carleton's scouts, Captain William McCleave, was captured by the Confederates and sent eastward to a Southern prison. Learning of this, Carleton ordered Lieutenant Colonel J. R. West to move from Fort Yuma toward Tucson by way of the Gila Trail. When West arrived at the Pima villages with a large scouting force, he heard of a Confederate detachment some thirty miles to the south at a former stage station on the Butterfield route; this was at Picacho Peak, a landmark on the Gila Trail where water was to be found. The federal commander quickly sent Lieutenant James Barrett with a dozen troops to capture these rebels. The result was the Battle of Picacho Pass, fought on April 15, 1862, won by the Confederates. Nevertheless, the battle availed them little, for from prisoners taken at the engagement Captain Hunter learned of the approach of the California Column; he knew his small force could not stand off an army of that size and made preparations for a retreat. The Battle of Picacho Pass represented the westernmost thrust of the Confederacy, but afterward the Southerners retreated in haste across the Gila Trail toward the safety of Texas.[19]

General Sibley, the man who sent Hunter to Tucson, meanwhile was achieving the same result: victory on the battlefield but over-all defeat. Moving northward from Mesilla up the Rio Grande Valley, his Army of New Mexico arrived on February 21 at Fort Craig for its contest with Canby's troops. During the morning hours it appeared that the federals would win what would come to be known as the Battle of Valverde. Sibley, sensing defeat—and prob-

144

ably quite drunk—later wrote, "At 1:30 p.m., having become completely exhausted and finding myself no longer able to keep the saddle, I sent my aides and other staff officers to report to Colonel Green." This was Tom Green, who, although a clerk of the Texas Supreme Court in civilian life, knew only one military tactic: charge! This proved so effective that it turned the tide of battle and caused the volunteers in Canby's force to turn and run. In fact, Canby and his troops moved inside Fort Craig for protection, expecting total defeat, but that evening about seven o'clock General Sibley felt well enough to resume command of the Confederates— and his first order was to break off the engagement. Then, leaving Canby and the federals inside the fort, he marched his men up the Rio Grande.[20] Albuquerque and Santa Fe he took with ease, which left only Fort Craig and Fort Union, a supply post in northeastern New Mexico, yet in federal hands.

He thereupon determined to capture Fort Union, and for this purpose sent Colonel William Scurry and some one thousand men marching out from Santa Fe. On March 26-28 they encountered the enemy at Glorieta Pass and fought a lengthy battle against Union soldiers and volunteers from Colorado; the Southerners won this engagement, but during it their supply wagons were captured by the Northerners. Scurry therefore had no option but to retreat.

After this conflict General Sibley had to face hard reality. Coming down the Santa Fe Trail, he knew, were more Union soldiers, to be reinforced by volunteers coming south from Colorado. Down the Rio Grande from Santa Fe was General Canby, still at Fort Craig with his army. And moving east from California was General Carleton and his California Column. Sibley knew he could stay and fight, but would lose; thus he had to order a retreat, although his men had won every battle they had fought. By April of 1862 Confederate New Mexico had ceased to exist. Sherrod Hunter likewise retreated toward Texas from Tucson as did Governor Baylor at Mesilla—and Confederate Arizona also was no more.

As the Confederates retreated, Union General Carleton advanced. The first unit to reach Tucson over the Gila Trail going east was that led by Colonel West, who arrived in May. Then in

145

June came the rest of the California Column. Carleton and his men marched through heat and choking dust, drinking foul water and eating bad food, sweating and cursing. There in Tucson on June 8 Carleton issued his proclamation to the people in the region: "In the present chaotic state in which Arizona is to be found: with no civil officers to administer the laws: indeed with an utter absence of all civil authority: and with no security of life or property within its borders: it becomes the duty of the undersigned to represent the authority of the United States. . . ." In short, he named himself governor of a territory with exactly the same borders as those announced by Baylor, all of present New Mexico and Arizona south of the 34th parallel.[21]

Carleton insisted that all people in Arizona take the oath of allegiance to the United States, that they have a lawful occupation, and that no words or deeds against the federal government would be tolerated. He taxed merchants to pay the expenses of his men, with a very heavy tax on gamblers and saloon-keepers to be used to care for his sick and wounded soldiers. Then, with southern Arizona securely under Union control, Carleton made preparations to link up with Canby in New Mexico. On July 4 he sent the first group of his men, 26 of them, marching east across the Gila Trail bound for Mesilla. On June 15 he sent two soldiers and a Mexican guide with messages to General Canby to tell what had happened; three days later in the vicinity of Apache Pass, east of Tucson, however, the three men were attacked by Indians. Sergeant William Wheeling and the Mexican guide, named Chavez, were killed, but Expressman John Jones was able to outride the attackers and reached the Rio Grande in safety—only to be captured by the Confederates and sent east to a military prison. In some unexplained manner, however, he was able to send the dispatches through to Canby, who no doubt was heartened to receive Carleton's message, "The Column from California is really coming."[22]

On June 21, not yet knowing the fate of his messengers to Canby, Carleton ordered Colonel Edward E. Eyre and 140 of his men to march east over the Gila Trail toward New Mexico. The same pattern repeated itself: the column had no difficulty until it

146

reached Apache Pass and the water hole there. As they watered their horses, a guard fired his rifle four times, a warning that Indians were approaching. These were Chiricahua Apaches from Cochise's band, and one of them came forward under a flag of truce. Eyre and his interpreter moved out, also under a flag of truce, where the colonel told the Indian that the soldiers "wish to be friends with the Apaches; at present, we are only traveling through your country and desire that you do not interfere with our men or animals. . . ." The Indian responded that he also wished to be friends, but when Eyre returned to his camp he learned that three of his men who had strayed from the camp had been shot and lanced. And that night shots were fired into the camp, but no attack came in force.[23] Eventually the column reached the Rio Grande, raising the Stars and Stripes at Fort Thorn (north of Mesilla) on July 4.

Carleton, apparently unhappy at the repeated attacks at Apache Pass, sent Captain Thomas L. Roberts with twenty-two wagons and two companies of troops on July 8 to establish a fort at that point. When Cochise's Apaches attacked, they were astonished to have howitzers open fire on them; after several hours of hard fighting they broke and fled, leaving the field to the Americans. However, Captain Roberts chose to escort a federal wagon train across the road rather than stay at Apache Pass.[24]

Finally Carleton himself marched east from Tucson with the majority of his army. Departing on July 20, 21, and 23, these troops reached the Rio Grande safely by August 7. Soon part of his army was probing into western Texas trying to make contact with the rebels. However, Texas would remain securely within the Confederate camp until the end of the Civil War in 1865.

Carleton's territory of Arizona, like Baylor's, proved difficult to administer, but he ruled with a heavy hand (which earned for him the nickname "Mogul"). His greatest problem was not Southern sympathizers, but the Indians. Just as Baylor before him, Carleton did not have enough troops and thus had to rely on volunteers to do battle with the Indians. He sent one such group under the command of Kit Carson against the Navajos; his instructions to

147

Carson were, "All Indian men of that tribe are to be killed whenever and wherever you find them; the women and children will not be harmed, but you will take them prisoners." Carson pursued a winter campaign in 1863-64 that broke the Navajo's proud spirit and saw that tribe relocated at the Bosque Redondo, a reservation-prison in east-central New Mexico.[25]

To Colonel J. R. West fell the task of contending with the Apaches, especially the Mimbreños, who lived along the eastern part of the Gila River. During the campaign waged by West, Mimbreño chieftain Mangas Coloradas was captured. According to West's report, Mangas was killed while rushing his guards. However, one of the soldiers who was there, Daniel E. Connor, later wrote that Colonel West had told the guards, "Men, that old murderer has got away from every soldier command and has left a trail of blood for five hundred miles on the old stage line. I want him dead or alive tomorrow morning, do you understand. *I want him dead.*" The next morning the prisoner was found dead. His death caused the Mimbreños to go on the reservation or else flee to the west and join with more warlike Apaches where they would fight to the death before surrendering their proud way of life and their lands.[26]

Carleton's harsh tactics did win a measure of peace along the Gila Trail, at least temporarily. But the greatest change as a result of the Civil War was political, not military, for in far-off Washington the politicians were debating the future of the region. General Carleton's proclamation of a territory of Arizona separate from New Mexico had been made without authorization; now the Congress would decide the issue. Early in April of 1862 a bill was introduced in the House of Representatives in Washington to separate Arizona and New Mexico, but on a line running from north to south, not east to west. John S. Watts, the territorial delegate from New Mexico, gave his support to the measure, even at one point attempting to describe Arizona to his fellow congressmen: "An Italian sunset never threw its gentle rays over more lovely valleys or heaven-killing hills, valleys harmonious with the music of a thousand sparkling rills, mountains shining with untold millions of

148

mineral wealth, wooing the hand of capital and labor to possess and use it." The House passed the bill on May 8, 1862, but in the Senate almost a year was needed before it finally was approved on February 20, 1863. President Abraham Lincoln signed the measure four days later. Thus if there was any winner in the Southwest during the Civil War, it was Arizona—which gained separate political status.[27]

But all the Southwest had lost heavily during this conflict, for mining virtually ceased and the stagecoaches did not roll across the Gila Trail, nor did the freight wagons. At the outbreak of the war the Butterfield Overland Mail had halted its run across the route it had pioneered; it moved to the north to follow a road directly west from St. Louis to Salt Lake City and San Francisco, leaving the Southwest without commercial transportation. Russell, Majors and Waddell, likewise had transferred its operations to the northern route, and even the smaller freighting companies had been forced to suspend operations. And in the quarrel between North and South, some men had been forced to make a choice of loyalty that tested them to the utmost. The war did not bring an "Eden of Liberty," but rather disruption, disorder, and disaster.

7

Reopening the Road

The arrival of Captain Sherrod Hunter and his two hundred Confederate "Arizona Volunteers" in Tucson of February 28, 1862, met with shouts of approval from most of the citizens who gathered to witness the event—but not from the Union sympathizers in the audience. The people who were "Secesh," or strong pro-Southern, were only a minority, while an equally small number were outspokenly Northern in their outlook; the majority of the citizens were shouting not because they were political but because they were delighted to see any armed body of men arrive who might contain the raiding Apaches. Among the small group of known "U.S. men," as they were called, was Estevan Ochoa, the freighter and merchant. Inasmuch as Ochoa did not remain silent, he soon came to the attention of Captain Hunter.

The Confederate officer had the freighter brought before him and said, "Mr. Ochoa, you realize, of course, that the United States no longer exists. I trust that you will yield to the new order, and take the oath of allegiance to the Confederacy. . . ." Otherwise, concluded Hunter, he would have to confiscate all of Ochoa's property and expel him from the city.

This threat of expulsion was not to be taken lightly, for outside the protection of the town a man was subject to quick death at the hands of the enraged followers of Cochise. And anyone expelled would have to travel either to northern New Mexico or else to California to reach the safety of Union lines. Despite Hunter's threat of expulsion and confiscation, Ochoa was steadfast: "It is out of the question for me to swear allegiance to any party or power hostile to the United States government," he said, "for to that Government I owe all my prosperity and happiness. When, sir, do you wish me to leave?"

Estevan Ochoa, the freight king. *Courtesy Arizona Historical Society.*

The answer was "Immediately." Ochoa was allowed to take only one horse, weapons, and whatever provisions he could assemble quickly. That same day he rode out of town to the east. Unharmed he traveled the Gila Trail to Mesilla and then turned north up the Rio Grande finally to arrive at the safety of a Union-held fort in New Mexico. There he waited until the summer of 1862 when the arrival of the California Column allowed him to return to Tucson in some triumph and even to recover most of his property.

And the presence of Union soldiers in Arizona and New Mexico allowed mining to resume in the territory, especially after General Carleton sent his troops into the field against the Indians. In Arizona in 1862 the principal area of mining was south of Tucson near the old settlement of Tubac, and this became Ochoa's freighting headquarters in the months that followed; the miners needed supplies, and his wagons brought them—at a profit. Then in 1863 came gold discoveries in northwestern Arizona, and the men who rushed there likewise needed supplies. Ochoa's wagons soon were rolling west to California and east to Santa Fe across the Gila Trail to bring the food and equipment needed.

Needing capital to expand, Ochoa in 1863 formed a partnership with P. R. Tully, creating the firm of Tully and Ochoa, and the following year they moved their main office from Tubac to Tucson. One other partner later would be added, Sydney R. DeLong, a Tucson merchant, after which the firm was known as Tully, Ochoa and Company. After the Civil War ended, this firm prospered to become the largest employer of men in any industry except mining in the Southwest. Kansas City was the major point at which Tully and Ochoa wagons picked up freight, after which it was brought to New Mexico by way of the Santa Fe Trail and then into Arizona over the Gila Trail. At one time the firm owned $100,000 in teams, wagons, and buildings, for the partners found it cheaper to construct their own way-stations than to pay to stable their animals in rented quarters. And in addition to supplying their own stores and the needs of several mining companies, Tully and Ochoa saw the possibilities and advantages of the international trade with Mexico, and their wagons began regularly rolling into Sonora and

152

Chihuahua. Finally, they signed contracts with the federal government to carry freight to Indian reservations and to the army posts
scattered through southern Arizona.

Their greatest losses as businessmen were not occasioned by
the weather or by the natural hazards of freighting but rather from
the depredations of the unhappy Apaches in the region. The worst
such attack came in May 1869. On the tenth of that month Santa
Cruz Castañeda, a Tully and Ochoa wagonmaster, set out from
Tucson bound for Camp Grant (in east-central Arizona); in this
train were nine wagons, eighty mules, and fourteen men. One day's
journey east of Tucson across the Gila Trail brought them to
Cañada del Oro; there they were attacked by an estimated two
hundred Apaches. Castañeda quickly had his men circle the wagons
and bring the mules inside, and they prepared to defend themselves
to the best of their ability.

The Apaches had no desire to attack this formation unless it
proved necessary, and they sent an emissary forward, one who
spoke Spanish. He told Castañeda that the Apaches did not desire
to kill the teamsters, that all they wanted was the goods; thus they
would allow the men to depart in peace if they would leave everything behind. The wagonmaster replied, "You can have the train
when we are no longer able to hold it." The fight was on.

For ten hours the Indians battled to take the circle, but from
behind their barricade the teamsters fought desperately. However,
at the end of this time Castañeda's situation was extremely serious.
Three of his men were dead, and his ammunition was getting very
low. At this moment seven soldiers rode into view, cavalry troopers
on their way from Camp Grant to Tucson. The soldiers charged,
but were driven off by intense fire from the Indians. The sergeant
then signaled Castañeda that the wagons should be abandoned, for
nothing more could be done. The wagonmaster and his men thereupon made a dash from their circle, joined the soldiers, and rode
madly toward Tucson. As they looked back they could see that the
Indians had set the wagons afire. This one incident alone cost Tully
and Ochoa an estimated $12,000.

Despite such losses, the firm prospered, and Ochoa became a

wealthy man. As such he became actively interested in the government of the town and the territory, serving in the upper house of the territorial legislature for several years. In this capacity Ochoa was largely responsible for the public school law enacted in 1871. That same year, at age forty, he married, and for his young bride he built a mansion that became the social center of Tucson. To it came almost all the leading visitors to Arizona, there to be entertained and housed.[1]

Other freighting firms competed in the Southwest with Tully, Ochoa and Company for the post-Civil War business generated by mining and the army, but this firm remained the largest and best known. The dust of their wagons mixed and mingled with that of the stage lines which were re-established at the close of the Civil War, for people and the mails likewise were crossing the Gila Trail again when the Confederacy died.

Prior to that conflict the Butterfield Overland Mail had crossed the region regularly and efficiently despite criticism in northern California's newspapers about the "Oxbow route" followed from St. Louis to San Francisco. In fact, by 1860 almost every Butterfield stage was crowded to capacity with passengers and mail, so that the pilgrim who grew tired and got off at some out-of-the-way station to get a good night's sleep might have to wait weeks before a coach came by—in either direction—with an empty seat. Service did deteriorate noticeably after John Butterfield stepped down as president of the Overland Mail in 1860 to be succeeded by William B. Dinsmore.

By the time Congress met in December 1860, critics of the Oxbow route were joined by a sufficient number of Northerners to ensure the shifting of the road. A bill to force the postmaster-general to employ a central route directly west from St. Joseph, Missouri, to Sacramento, California, cleared both houses on March 12, but already the Gila Trail route had been closed. Six days earlier the Overland had ceased to try to cross the Southwest because of Confederate raids on their livestock, rolling stock, and stations.[2] Four months later, on July 18, 1861, the stages began moving west from St. Joseph, Missouri (at the end of the Hannibal and St.

154

A wagon train under Indian attack on the plains. *From Harper's Weekly.*

A Butterfield stage leaving Atchison, Kansas. *From Harper's Weekly.*

Joseph Railroad), to Folsom, California (where a short-line railroad connected with Sacramento). Already Dinsmore had despaired of continuing the service and had sub-contracted most of this service to the Central Overland California and Pike's Peak Express Company, which was to carry the mail from Missouri to Salt Lake City; and at the western end, Dinsmore sub-contracted with the Pioneer Stage Line to carry the mail from Virginia City, Nevada, to Sacramento.

The central route proved satisfactory during the summer of 1861, but as fall and winter approached the stages moved slower and slower—until snow virtually halted their movement. By the spring of 1862 the Central Overland Company and Pike's Peak Express Company was at the edge of bankruptcy, as were its owners, the firm of Russell, Majors and Waddell (which had ruined itself on the costly experiment known as the Pony Express). Purchasing this firm was Ben Holladay, who would come to be known as the "Napoleon of the Plains." Born in Kentucky in 1824, Holladay had run away from home to try saloonkeeping, working in a general store, and carrying the mail before he entered the field of transportation. The Mexican War saw him in the freighting business in the Southwest, and then loans to Russell, Majors and Waddell saw his acquisition of that firm early in 1862.[3]

With this acquisition, Holladay entered the passenger business in a determined way. By 1866 his stages were running from Missouri to Nevada, north into Montana, and through the Rocky Mountains from Denver to Salt Lake City. Eventually he would operate more than five thousand miles of stage service, along with his freighting endeavors and his steamships running to Oregon, Panama, and the Orient. This complex he organized extensively, a superintendent in charge of each two hundred miles of stage line and a conductor riding every coach. From this he made large sums of money, which he spent lavishly on his homes in White Plains, New York, and Washington, D.C., along with loans to prospectors and donations for civil improvement in the West.[4]

In all of this Holladay had only one real competitor, the firm of Wells, Fargo and Company. William B. Dinsmore, president of

William G. Fargo, of Wells, Fargo fame. *From Harper's Monthly.*

A stagecoach used in Arizona in the early 1880s.
Courtesy Arizona Historical Society.

the Overland Mail Company, eventually had given way to William G. Fargo, and he in turn had merged this remainder of John Butterfield's dream into his own firm of Wells, Fargo and Company. This company had been incorporated in 1852 in the state of New York, but its principal purpose was to move gold, as well as mail, in the mineral country in California. By 1860 it dominated the express business in the entire state, gradually moving into the stagecoaching business, especially after it absorbed the remains of the Overland Mail Company.[5]

These two giants of western stagecoaching might have quarreled or even come to rate wars. However, Holladay realized that the transcontinental railroad then under construction would replace his stages as a means of transportation, and on November 1, 1866, he sold his holdings to Wells, Fargo for $1,500,000 plus $300,000 of Wells, Fargo stock and a seat on their board of directors.[6] The owners of this firm also saw that the transcontinental railroad would hurt the staging business, but they gambled that such a railroad could not be completed for another ten years. It took only three! However, Wells, Fargo stages did provide a transcontinental overland method of travel until that time, and after 1869 they provided transportation to towns not served by the railroad. Gradually their business was reduced until at last they were only in banking and express service.

In the immediate post-Civil War years, however, neither Holladay nor Wells, Fargo ran coaches through the Southwest, for there were too few passengers to justify the cost. Not until 1869 did stages rumble and bounce across the Gila Trail once again; that year the Southern Overland U. S. Mail and Express opened service between Tucson, Mesilla, El Paso, and eastward into Texas. Then in 1870 came the Tucson, Arizona City, and San Diego Stage Company, which re-established service from Arizona to the West Coast and thereby completed a transcontinental link to carry people and mail across this region. These firms, with various reorganizations, would continue to operate until 1881 and the completion of the transcontinental railroad.

Driving these coaches with their four- and six-horse teams was

159

a difficult job, one not learned readily even by young men raised to drive the family wagon or family buggy. The person employed to drive a Butterfield or a Wells, Fargo or Southern Overland stage needed to know how to handle three sets of reins simultaneously with the left hand; the right hand had to be free to take up slack or to wield the whip kept in a socket on the right side of the driver's box. He had to be able to coax half-wild mustangs in the intricacy of a turn, for if the lead team, swing (middle) team, and wheelers (rear team) did not coordinate their efforts they would tangle, injuring themselves and even, on occasion, upsetting the coach. Thus the task called for experience, strength, coolness, and an ability to curse in such a way as to command the attention of both mules and mustangs.

These men, some of them former teamsters, others from the farms, and yet others from a diversity of backgrounds, saw themselves as knights of the road without peer in the land. An English traveler, commenting on American stage drivers, noted that such men felt "inferior to no one in the Republic," and that "even the President, were he on board, must submit to his higher authority." In their driving these men reflected their individual personalities: some were cautious, some friendly, some insane. They were little more than vagabonds at heart, moving from one part of the country to another for no reason other than curiosity or whim. Few of these men drank on duty, however, for they realized their profession demanded intelligence, quickness, and a clear head. Nine lives—those of the passengers inside the coach—were dependent on the driver, ten if he had a passenger beside him on the box (and this was the seat of honor, reserved for the most distinguished ticket-holder of the day).

Thus seated on his box, a chew of tobacco in his mouth, his whip at his right hand, the driver was a man among men, the idol of young boys who listened for his bugle to blow at the edge of town so they could rush to the depot and admire him. In the words of a modern song, the stage driver was "king of the road."

Also crossing the Southwest following the Civil War were renewed cattle drives. In the immediate aftermath of the war, Texans

160

had little cash but plenty of longhorn cattle. These beasts had run wild since the earliest days of Spanish settlement in the Rio Grande Valley of south Texas and by 1865 numbered between 3 and 6 million—worth only $4 or $5 in Texas but $40 to $50 in the industrializing North. The long trail drive was born to connect the $4 cow with the $40 market. By 1867 the Chisholm Trail was a reality as longhorns were driven north to the railhead at Abilene, Kansas.

At the same time cattle were being driven westward into New Mexico and Arizona, where ranching was being reorganized following the end of the Civil War. There had been a few large cattle ranches in these two areas in the 1850s, but Indian raids had ended these pioneering efforts. Then with the return of soldiers and the creation of reservations, ranching could spread once again—for both soldiers and Indians, along with the miners, had to be fed. Thus cattle were crossing the Gila Trail both to stock ranches and to supply the beef needs of Indians on the reservations and soldiers at the army posts.

One of the most famous of the early cattlemen to arrive in Arizona in the 1860s was Henry Clay Hooker, a refugee from the California gold rush. In 1866, his hardware store in Placerville, California, had burned, leaving him with only about $1000 and a wife and three children to feed. This money he used to purchase 500 turkeys at $1.50 apiece; then with one helper and several dogs he drove these turkeys overland to the Nevada mining camps where they sold for $5 apiece. Hooker used these profits to enter the cattle business in Arizona; in 1867 he secured a contract to supply beef to army posts in the northern part of the territory, as well as to several reservations. He owned no ranch of his own; rather he would go to Texas, purchase the cattle he needed to fill a contract, and drive them to Arizona by way of the Gila Trail.

On one occasion Hooker came face to face with the Indians, but not those on the reservation. In April 1870 he was driving by buggy to Fort Bowie to speak with the post commander about a beef contract. He sat in the front seat, a Winchester rifle across his lap and a six-shooter in a holster mounted on the buggy dashboard; seated in the rear of the wagon, facing backward, was an employee

161

Henry C. Hooker, a pioneer rancher. *Courtesy Arizona Historical Society*.

who had a double-barreled shotgun cradled in his arms and a six-shooter in a holster in his belt. In this fashion Hooker and his helper could look forward and backward and not be surprised. On this occasion they were not taken unaware, but were surrounded by so many Chiricahua Apaches that they could not fight their way clear or outrun them. Hooker's decision was quick; he turned the team and headed straight for the mountains to the south, a range known all across the Southwest as the Cochise Stronghold.

Arriving at the Indian village hidden deep in these mountains, Hooker calmly got out of the wagon and sat in front of the chief's wickiup. Eventually, Cochise himself came into the camp, and food was placed before the two men. Afterward Hooker was shown where to sleep. The next morning he again was fed, and then his wagon and weapons were brought to him. As he prepared to depart, he asked Cochise, out of curiosity, why he had not been killed. Cochise replied that the rancher had been treated courteously because he brought cattle to Arizona for the Indians to eat. Unlike other whites he did not try to hurt the Indians or take their land, and thus had been left in peace. Hooker then departed to arrive at Fort Bowie a day late—but healthy. On his next trip to northern Arizona, he had a Navajo make a bright red blanket for the Apache chief with the word Cochise woven into the center of it. At his deathbed in 1874, Cochise indicated his desire to be buried in this blanket.

In 1872 Hooker used the profits he had made trailing beef into Arizona over the Gila Trail to establish the Sierra Bonita Ranch in the Sulphur Springs Valley of southeastern Arizona. Within a few years he had the largest and most successful ranch in the territory. It was he who introduced the new breeds of cattle—shorthorns, Durhams, and Herefords—to the region, and on the 800 square miles of territory he controlled he entertained the many guests who came to his spread.[7]

Other men realized the same profits from trailing Texas cattle westward, fattening them on Arizona or New Mexican grass, and then marketing them locally. John H. Slaughter, the Texan who in the 1880s would tame the boom town of Tombstone, started his

163

Right.
John H. Slaughter,
rancher and sheriff
of Cochise County.
Courtesy Arizona Historical Society.

Below.
A rear view of
John H. Slaughter's home
at the San Bernardino Ranch.
Courtesy Arizona Historical Society.

ranch on an old Spanish land grant of 40,000 acres in southeastern Arizona,[8] while John Chisum worked in eastern New Mexico; in fact, Chisum's empire in the Pecos River Valley extended some 150 miles up the Pecos from the Texas border to Fort Sumner, and his herd was estimated at 60,000 head of cattle.

Cattle barons such as Hooker, Slaughter, and Chisum employed hundreds of cowboys, and they, like the miners, farmers, and townspeople of the Southwest, wrote letters to be carried by stagecoach, and they needed supplies from the East. All these residents knew they were not getting the same mail service as were residents of other parts of the West, and naturally they wanted to see improvements. Particularly they wanted a way to get news bulletins and commercial facts faster than by mail, which required ten to fifteen days from St. Louis and at least seven days from Los Angeles. True, they wanted a railroad built that would give them freight and passenger service, but even more they wanted—and needed—to be connected to the outside world by the telegraph.

Samuel F. B. Morse had perfected this instrument in 1844, and shortly thereafter it had been demonstrated publicly. Gradually the "talking wires" had been strung down the coast from San Francisco to Los Angeles, but had not started eastward toward Arizona prior to the end of the Civil War. Governor Richard C. McCormick asked members of the fifth legislature to send a memorial to Congress asking for funds with which to build a telegraph across the territory. But it would be the army, not civilians, who strung the wires along the Gila Trail.

At the end of the Civil War, the land along the Gila Trail was still largely an Indian domain. San Diego, Yuma, Tucson, and Mesilla were lonely outposts of American settlement, islands of safety in a sea of Indian control. To force these natives onto reservations, the army began reorganizing after fighting ended in the East. On January 20, 1865, Arizona was separated from the Department of New Mexico and placed under the military Department of California. To this district in the next six years came several commanders, but they accomplished little other than establishing several isolated army posts; the troops at these forts were

165

out of communication except by messenger service, and word of Indian outbreaks often did not reach them in time for the soldiers to react effectively. By 1870 the situation was so desperate that Arizona was severed from California and made a separate department, and the following year command of it was given to Lieutenant Colonel George Crook, the man most responsible for the building of a telegraph in the Southwest.

A West Point graduate and a major general during the Civil War, Crook was an unusual soldier. Wearing a weather-beaten canvas suit and a Japanese summer hat, he traveled to all parts of Arizona with no military trappings of any sort, not even a symbol of his rank. His first annual report from Arizona stressed that his greatest need was for quick communication between his forts. He wrote, "Owing to the isolated condition of this department, and the scattered distribution of its posts, the construction of a telegraph-line from California to this country, with branches to some of the important posts, would not only be of great service, but be economy to the Government." His commanding officer, General John M. Schofield, who had charge of the Division of the Pacific, added an endorsement to this, stating that the state of communications between his headquarters and Arizona was "a source of embarrassment, delay, and expense." Likewise, the commanding general of the army, William T. Sherman, endorsed Crook's need of the telegraph. Still nothing was done.

Again in his annual report of 1872, Colonel Crook stated his need: "There can be no doubt that the establishment of telegraphic communication with all the important points in the territory with the connecting lines outside, would be an advantage to the public service too great to be estimated." Because of this interest at high levels in the army, the matter of a military telegraph into Arizona was assigned to the acting quartermaster general for the Division of the Pacific, Lieutenant Colonel Robert O. Tyler.

A severely wounded veteran of the Civil War, Tyler started to work on this project in November 1871. First he approached the general superintendent of Western Union's Pacific Division, James Gamble. Gamble said that Western Union could build the line, but was not interested in operating it because there were too few people in Arizona to justify it as a commercial venture. The two men, working together, mapped the approach to be used. From Yuma to the mountains just east of San Diego, there was no timber available for poles; cottonwood poles could be secured along the Gila River for 75 miles east of Yuma, these to be cut and floated down the river to where they were needed. They estimated needing 20 poles to the mile at a cost of $1 each; wire for each mile would cost $60, glass insulators per mile would total $12, and another $10 per mile would be needed to pay all other costs. This brought a grand total of $242 per mile of telegraph, or $150,000 for linking all army posts in Arizona to San Diego. Of course, said Gamble, the cost would be less if the army did the work.

Tyler next figured the cost with army work crews, a reduced number of poles per mile of 17, iron wire at $30 per mile, and insulators at $.25 each; his new figure was $52.95 per mile for construction. With an addition of 25 per cent to this budget for transportation, tools, and incidental expenses plus four telegraph stations, Tyler arrived at a final budget of $50,311.80 for 628 miles of telegraph (lines running along the Gila Trail to Tucson and north to Prescott, Arizona, as well as to all army posts in the territory). With endorsements by General Schofield, this report was forwarded to the secretary of war, who sent it to Congress early in 1872 with a request that the money be appropriated.

Former Governor Richard C. McCormick, in 1872 the territorial delegate to Congress from Arizona, spoke on behalf of this bill when it came before the House on January 30, 1872. Other Arizonans happily wrote Congress to plead for passsage of this measure, and editorials warmly applauded it; for example, the *Weekly Arizona Miner*, a newspaper in Prescott, stated on March 9, 1872, that with passage of this measure "soldiers and citizens of our territory will no doubt have the pleasure of hearing quickly the important news of the 'outside world.' " More than a year was required before Congress voted on the measure, however, but the vote was favorable; Congressman James Garfield of Ohio introduced the resolution that became law on March 3, 1873, with the

167

funds to become available on July 1 that year.

Contracts quickly were made with civilian companies for providing the telegraph instruments, insulators, and wire, while R. R. Haines, manager of the Western Union office in Los Angeles, was hired as superintendent of construction. Working on the project for the army would be Captain George F. Price, who had first entered the army as part of the California Column. Soon the survey began, every town wanting to be on the route, some of them even donating poles in order to have the line run through the vicinity. Yet the route could not swerve far away from the Gila Trail and the government wagon road, for water was available along it. The only major change was to run the wire through the small city of Phoenix, which was growing rapidly in central Arizona. The major difficulty which the surveyors encountered was the shifting sand west of Yuma; there was no water along this route, and the blowing sand would make the placing of poles very uncertain. This survey was completed on August 2, 1873, with Haines and Price certain that the construction would take only five months.

Yuma became the central point for the building of this line, for wire and all other materials could be brought by ship to the mouth of the Colorado River and up it by barge to be placed at Yuma. Troop labor teams then were assigned, each team to work a hundred miles or more. Captain Price himself took charge of the team locating the wire from Oatman Flat to Maricopa Wells to Tucson.

The first pole was put in the ground at San Diego on August 28 with little fanfare. At Prescott, Arizona, however, the setting of the first pole was the occasion of a public ceremony; Colonel Crook was present, and it was his wife who turned the first shovel of earth. Work then got under way in earnest. Although the army teams were not members of the Signal Corps, and thus had no experience at building a telegraph, their work nevertheless proceeded rapidly. By November 11 the line was complete from Yuma to Prescott, and among the first messages to go over the wire was a notice that George Crook had been promoted to brigadier general for his spectacular service in the Indian wars. Exactly a week later, Yuma and

Above.
The building of the telegraph.
Courtesy Library of Congress.

Left.
Stringing a military telegraph.
Courtesy Library of Congress.

San Diego were linked. Finally, with as much as 13 miles of wire being strung in a single day, Tucson was reached on December 2, the final connection made at 10:00 a.m. Price wired the editors of the newspaper at San Diego, "The Arizona military telegraph is completed. The wire now connects San Diego with her 'back country.'" To this he added a bit of verse:

> The lightning message of thought
> Obeys man's proud decree
> And mountains, answering, echo back
> The voices from the sea.

The captain's final report showed that 540 miles of telegraph had been built, using 9820 poles, in just 97 days. The cost of all this, including almost 100 miles of wire and 1000 brackets and insulators left over, was just $45,557.97.

In 1874 came more money from Congress for extending the telegraph through Arizona to other army posts such as Camp Verde and Camp Apache. Eventually every army post and every reservation in the territory was connected by telegraph, bringing about greater efficiency in halting Indian outbreaks, making possible rapid movements of troops in pursuit of renegades, and reducing Indian raids.

In fact, this line was so successful from a military point of view that Congress on March 3, 1875, authorized the construction of a line from Tucson to Santa Fe (where the line from Missouri ended). Again troop labor would be used to cut the cost of construction. In charge of this construction was Lieutenant Philip Reade, who began work in July that year. The route he chose was Cooke's Wagon Road: down the Rio Grande to Mesilla and then west to Tucson. The specifications drawn by Lieutenant Reade called for 25 poles to the mile, each pole to be of quality-grade wood, and the insulators and wire to be of top quality. However, funds for this project soon ran out and work halted by early 1876.

Lieutenant Reade was not discouraged. If he could not buy the poles he needed, he would beg them. And beg he did. At meetings with citizens in Arizona he said that local residents there had

170

the cheapest telegraph rates in the United States thanks to the army's work, and he taunted them, "If continued telegraphic communications be desired, it behooves the citizens to be no less public-spirited than our New Mexican neighbors." He told them that at similar meetings in New Mexico he had received numerous pledges: 200 poles from Silver City, 625 poles from Balencia County, 1000 poles at half cost from Bernalillo County, and $1500 from residents at Las Cruces and Mesilla—with local farmers all along the way pledging to use their oxen and wagons to haul the poles free of charge. The editor of the Tucson *Citizen* added his challenge to Arizona's residents: "In New Mexico the press, the people and the military combined to help along an enterprise, governmental in nature, but essentially by the people and for the people. Will Arizona do likewise?" The people did; from Tucson came a pledge of 900 poles.

These pledges in hand, Reade was able to continue work although Congress failed to appropriate money for the project. By April the Tucson *Citizen* was able to announce that completion of the southern overland telegraph was near at hand. This prediction came true during the first week of May 1877. Arizona and New Mexico were linked together, completing the line from the Pacific coast at San Diego to the Gulf of Mexico at Galveston and through the Midwest to St. Louis. The telegraph was a reality at last.

The operators who manned this line immediately became important members of each community in the Southwest, for the position required great integrity. The San Diego *Daily Union* noted the sensitive position the operator occupied: "He is the possessor of the earliest tidings of life or death, of war and rumors of war, of fire, flood and tempest, and frequently, of the weightiest secrets. He can tell many a tale of woe, error, sin, or shame. . . . His position is one of great difficulty, also, because he has a sacred charge to keep, and many are the temptations offered to induce a hint of his superior knowledge of the affairs of the men around. But, though bound by no oath and under no bond save that of honor, he rarely betrays his trust." Because the telegraph so quickly became a vital part of men's lives in the Southwest, the newspapers usually took note of

171

Currier and Ives print depicting the "progress of the century";
note the telegraph and the railroad. *Courtesy Library of Congress.*

the comings and goings of the operators, of repairs to the line, and of the general condition of service.

One of the most immediate uses of the telegraph was military. Soldiers were quickly notified of outbreaks from the reservations and of raids, and thus they could take the field in pursuit of renegades much sooner than they had previously. It was this factor which had caused General Crook to push so hard for completion of the line. At first the natives little understood the workings of the new instrument. In June of 1874 two White Mountain Apaches came off their reservation to spend a week in Prescott; during that time they were shown the new telegraph office, and while there saw a message come in about an army attack on an Indian village. They were not convinced of the truth of this until they had walked five miles out of town following the wire. Upon their return they were given an electric shock from the line. They left the office, reported the operator, "with mingled fear and disgust."

It did not take the Indians long to understand fully the nature of the new instrument, however. By 1885, when Geronimo led renegades off the San Carlos Reservation, one of their first acts was to cut the telegraph line and splice the cut together with rawhide; the splice was made with such attention to detail that many hours were required to find it—hours during which the hostiles got a long jump on pursuing soldiers.

Civilian commerce likewise benefitted greatly from the telegraph. The rates charged for use of the military telegraph were considerably lower than those charged by Western Union elsewhere in the country, and goods and freight moved more readily as a result. Likewise the newspapers found it beneficial; all across the Southwest they soon had a section entitled "Telegraphic News" which contained the latest national and world news. Because of the telegraph it soon was possible to have daily newspapers rather than the weeklies which had sufficed to chronicle local events.

Another role played by the telegraph was aid in apprehending criminals. Distance no longer became the safety of men outside the law. For example, in July of 1876 three men stole some horses in Phoenix and then rode rapidly southward toward the Mexican

173

border, hoping to escape American lawmen by crossing the international boundary. However, by telegraph the sheriff in Tucson was warned that the thieves probably would pass through the area and to be on the watch for them. This proved a good prediction, for soon after the telegram came the sheriff's deputies found three men fitting the description of the criminals riding across the open ground east of Tucson. They were arrested, returned to Phoenix, and brought to trial—"cursing the telegraph." Other criminals in New Mexico and Arizona soon learned to fear the rapid spread of news of their misdeeds, for the telegraph certainly traveled faster than a horse.

The military telegraph thus brought widespread benefits to the Southwest.[9] Yet its day was brief, for inching across the region were steel rails—which were paralleled by strands of wire for a commercial telegraph. One by one the military sections of the telegraph closed as the commercial rival opened service. By 1882 the army's line from San Diego to Yuma had been abandoned, the materials it left to be used for repairs elsewhere or else taken up and used to string wire to very isolated posts in the general region. Within two years after this, the last major link with the outside world was being manned by civilians, not soldiers, and the military telegraph ceased to be a major instrument flashing messages along the Gila Trail.

While the telegraph, military and civilian, served to bring rapid communication to the Southwest, it was no instrument for conveying goods. By the mid-1870s, freight was still being moved by the cumbersome wagons that had served to bring supplies to the region in the 1850s. But the Civil War had settled the sectional conflict, and at last it was possible for a transcontinental railroad to be built.

8

Steel Rails at Last

In a way the father of the southern transcontinental railroad was Theodore D. Judah, usually called "Crazy Judah" in his own day. Judah went west to San Francisco in 1853 at the request of Charles L. Wilson, president of a firm known as the Sacramento Valley Rail Road Company. This company was incorporated in 1852 to run rails from Sacramento northeast to the gold diggings on the American River and beyond. Wilson wanted Judah as chief engineer of his line, for Judah had demonstrated his competence in the East by building a railroad bridge across Niagara gorge. Judah went west, and he actually laid track for the Sacramento Valley, track that snaked its way up the American River toward Folsom, California.

Finished with this task, Judah conceived the scheme that a railroad could be built through the Sierra to Nevada and the Great Basin country. Yet when he tried to raise money for this line in San Francisco, local residents dismissed him as a crank. When the Corps of Topographical Engineers conducted its surveys in 1853-54, however, it found that Judah's idea was sound: a railroad could be constructed between the 38th and 39th parallels, one running from St. Louis to Salt Lake City and San Francisco. Yet this line did not become an immediate reality because of the quarrel between North and South. Then in 1861 Southerners walked out of Congress, and it was free at last to act. On July 1, 1862, it chartered the Union Pacific Company to begin building westward, and the Central Pacific Company to begin building eastward along Crazy Judah's route.

There were so few people living along this route in 1862 that congressmen knew the building and operating of a railroad through the region would not be possible without a federal subsidy. After all, a railroad made its money from moving people and freight, and there were too few people along the right-of-way to make the route profitable. Thus Congress voted an inducement: (1) free right-of-way across public lands, (2) free use of minerals and timber with which to build the track, (3) 10 sections of public land to be given to the railroad for each mile of track laid, this land to be sold by the railroad to help pay for the cost of laying track, and (4) a loan of $16,000 per mile of track laid across the plains, a $32,000 loan per mile of track in the foothills of the West, and a $48,000 loan per mile of track laid in the mountains. When these inducements proved not enough to get the railroad track laid rapidly, Congress in 1864 doubled the amount of public land to be given to the Union and Central Pacific railroads to 20 sections of land per mile of track laid, and it said the loan money would be a second mortgage. With these inducements, the *building* of a railroad (not running one, just constructing it) became profitable.

Little work began in earnest on the two lines until after the Civil War. After that conflict ended, ample labor became available and financial support was then arranged. Oakes Ames of Massachusetts and his brother had devised a scheme for the making of fortunes by the directors of the Union Pacific. They set up a construction company, the Crédit Mobilier of America, whose main stockholders were the men on the board of directors of the Union Pacific; the board members of the Union Pacific then voted contracts for the construction of the railroad to their own construction company—at very high rates. The profits thus made they then divided among themselves. And when some congressman asked too many questions about the high cost of building the railroad, he was allowed to buy or was given shares of profitable Crédit Mobilier stock.

The four leaders of the Central Pacific Railroad saw the advantages of financing through this method, and soon they had their own construction company organized. Thereby they made fortunes for themselves in a very short time. Previously they had been poor merchants. Leland Stanford had been a grocer in Sacramento,

Charles Crocker a drygoods merchant, and Collis P. Huntington and Mark Hopkins partners in a hardware store. Judah had persuaded them of the soundness of his idea, and they in turn formed the Central Pacific, which secured the charter from Congress to build eastward from Sacramento. Thus they became the "Big Four" of California railroading. They divided the labor among themselves as track was laid: Huntington became the financial genius and purchasing agent; Hopkins served as treasurer and business manager; Crocker superintended construction; and Stanford, as governor of California, took care of political problems. They solved the problem of getting labor by importing large numbers of Chinese workers, paying them low wages to push track through the towering Sierra. By 1867 they emerged into the high desert of the Great Basin and began racing eastward at the rate of seven, eight, and even ten miles of track a day; President Lincoln earlier had generously called this high desert "mountains," and the large loan available from Congress made laying track here very profitable. The Union Pacific likewise was racing west over this desert, for it also wanted the profits. And both lines wanted to be first into the Mormon settlements to get their business.

So profitable was laying track in the Great Basin that by 1868 both the Union and Central Pacific's directors were talking of continuing across the country, laying two sets of track parallel to one another. Congress finally grew tired of this proposal, however, and decreed that the two lines should meet at Promontory Point, a small town west of Ogden, Utah. High company officials and honored guests gathered there on May 10, 1869, and a polished laurel tie bound with silver was put into place. Rails were brought forward, and the final spikes were driven. To President Grant in Washington went a telegram stating, "The last rail is laid, the last spike driven. The Pacific Railroad is completed."

Huntington, Stanford, Hopkins, and Crocker originally had intended only to build the Central Pacific, then sell it, making their profit from the construction of the line not from operating it. Because so much money had been invested in its building (much of it in the form of profits for the Big Four), no one was interested in

177

purchasing it in 1869. In order for them to operate the line at a profit, they therefore had to maintain a monopoly on railroading to California. To accomplish this, they incorporated several short lines and began laying track to key points in the state.

One of these short lines was called the Southern Pacific. It was chartered in the state of California to run from San Francisco down the coast to San Diego; the legislature granted this company right-of-way on state land and allowed it to collect bounties from the various counties and cities along the way. Work was pushed rapidly, for the Big Four wanted to reach Los Angeles and San Diego, then run spur lines east to Needles, California, and to Yuma, the two natural routes of entry for thirty-fifth- and thirty-second-parallel railroads.

And railroads along these two routes had been chartered by Congress. That body had chartered the Atlantic and Pacific Railroad on June 27, 1866, with authority to lay track from Springfield, Missouri, to Albuquerque, New Mexico, and then west along the 35th parallel "as near as may be found most suitable." However, this company failed to lay much track before going bankrupt in the Panic of 1873, during which it was bought out by the Atchison, Topeka and Santa Fe. That company, which had already reached Albuquerque by laying track from Kansas down the Santa Fe Trail, began building westward in May 1880. Northern Arizona proved difficult to cross, but by August of 1883 the track had reached the Colorado River just across from Needles, California. For a while further progress was halted as the owners of the Santa Fe dealt with the Big Four for right-of-way into California; an agreement was reached on August 20, 1884, and within a year the Santa Fe had reached the Pacific Coast.

The other transcontinental chartered by Congress, the Texas and Pacific, was to run along the 32nd parallel from Marshall in eastern Texas westward to San Diego. Chartered on March 3, 1871, this line made slow progress. In June 1872 Colonel Thomas A. Scott became its president, and gradually track was laid; on July 19, 1876, the first train reached Fort Worth. But the Panic of 1873 ruined Scott's ambitions of being a railroad baron; his funds were

178

Collis P. Huntington, the man most responsible for the Southern Pacific.
From The National Cyclopedia of American Biography (1914).

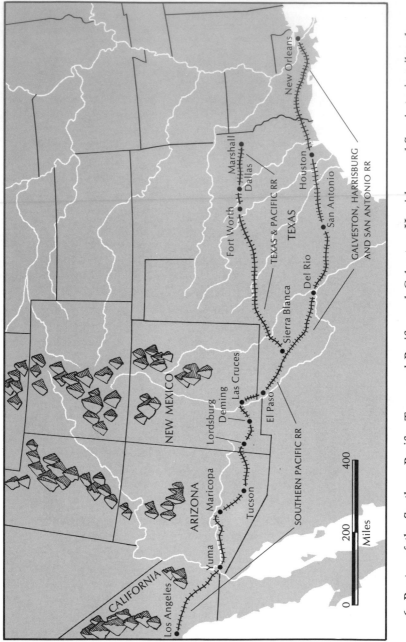

6. Routes of the Southern Pacific, Texas and Pacific, and Galveston, Harrisburg and San Antonio railroads.

gone, and he could not get federal funds until he reached El Paso and began building across New Mexico and Arizona. Thus he went to Washington to plead for aid, but Congress denied it to him. At the same time, Collis P. Huntington was in Washington representing the Southern Pacific; that line had built a spur east to Yuma over the western part of the Gila Trail, and Huntington wanted Congress to transfer the Texas and Pacific charter, with its federal subsidies, to his line for building across Arizona and New Mexico. Congress refused.

At this juncture Jay Gould entered the picture. Gould was a Wall Street financier and operator who had made a fortune on the stock market. He had little interest in operating railroads, but he did believe a fortune could be made in western railroading. Thus he approached Colonel Scott, who was glad to sell out. This brought on a clash between the Southern Pacific and its Big Four and Jay Gould and his Texas and Pacific.

Neither side wanted to lose money, however. All involved were businessmen who realized that by fighting all would lose, while cooperation probably would make money for everyone. Thus Gould met Huntington in New York, and there they decided to work together. Their agreement was that Gould would build west across Texas, while Huntington would push his Southern Pacific east from Yuma; the two lines then would meet in the vicinity of El Paso. Gould would give his federal subsidies for building across New Mexico and Arizona to the Southern Pacific, in return for which he would gain access to the West Coast over the Southern Pacific's track. The revenue generated by this transcontinental would be shared by all, much as were the profits made by the Union Pacific and the Central Pacific. Neither man trusted the other, but necessity dictated that they work together.

This agreement in hand, Huntington was ready to send his men into Arizona. Iron rails at last would span the historic Gila Trail in earnest. First came permission from Congress in 1877 to build across the Fort Yuma reservation, and then a bridge had to be constructed across the wide Colorado River. Yuma remained the terminus of the railroad for some eighteen months as Huntington sought aid from the territorial legislatures of Arizona and New Mexico. In fact, rumors persisted for years thereafter that the Southern Pacific baron sent $25,000 to Arizona to be used as bribes for members of the legislature and that Governor A. P. K. Safford subsequently returned $20,000 of the money to Huntington—after the measure had been passed—saying that only $5000 was needed to "buy" Arizona's legislature.[1]

Construction began eastward from Yuma in November 1878 following the Gila Trail. This was along bottom land adjacent to the Gila River. This work went forward rapidly during months that elsewhere in the country would have brought snow so deep as to halt progress, but the winter months were the most comfortable months for laying track across the desert Southwest. For the 252 miles to Tucson there were no towns at which supplies could be bought or where freight and passengers needed to be deposited. There were only the ruins of former way-stations for the Butterfield Overland Mail, so the workers had to make their own towns. And when the workers moved on, they left behind, along with their debris, little villages; these were a succession of ramshackle railhead towns that housed the Irish, Chinese, and other immigrant workers who drove the spikes and carried the ties, along with the merchants who had portable stores to supply them with goods, and the gamblers and saloonkeepers who came to separate them from their pay. These shanty towns in many ways were similar to the mining boom camps that had appeared in California during the gold rush, raw little eyesores made of canvas and green lumber. Each had a brief moment of glory as the railhead town, and then when the end-of-track moved too far east, most of the town would be loaded on freight cars and moved forward. In this way the buildings that had been Gila Bend in the morning became Casa Grande before nightfall. Once the workers and most of the buildings disappeared down the track, the remainder of the town left behind fell into a sharp depression bordering death, gradually to revive and become a freight depot for ranchers and farmers in the vicinity and to assume a new life with schools and churches and libraries and even jails.

182

The engineer in charge of building the line from Yuma to Tucson, William Hood, had the tracks follow the Gila River eastward to Adonde Wells, then twist through the Mohawk Mountains and through beds of lava, eventually to reach a site known as Maricopa, which was seven miles south of the old stage station known as Maricopa Wells. For a time it seemed that Maricopa would be an exception to the other end-of-track towns, that it would boom and grow; the land in the area was fertile, and a special train ran from California to bring prospective farmers to the area. Real estate promoters were the only buyers, however, for farming at Maricopa required a huge capital investment to put in the necessary irrigation canals. The bubble burst as quickly as it had risen, Maricopa slumped, and in 1887 the railroad moved both its offices and the town name four miles to the east.

At the original railroad town of Maricopa, engineer Hood began to curve the roadbed to the southeast. In fact, he laid out the longest curve in the history of railroading, five miles of continuous curve. Then, seemingly tired of what he had done, he followed this with one of the longest stretches of straight track in the world: forty-seven miles without a bend. Casa Grande had its moment of glory on May 19, 1879, when the track reached that point, but work then halted to await the passing of the hot summer months. Thus it was not until March 17, 1880, that track was laid to the depot of the Old Pueblo, as Tucson was known.

Tucson at this time was a town of some two thousand residents. The streets yet were of dirt, and in them dogs and hogs roamed at will, mixing with donkeys loaded with firewood and wagons loaded with freight. Drunken cowboys in town for a spree swore and fought with troops on leave from nearby Fort Lowell. Still visible in the town was the wall erected by Spanish soldiers of a century before to protect the townspeople from roving bands of Apaches. Yet by 1880 there were shade trees and spacious lawns around some of the better homes. An ice plant was operating to make summer a little more bearable, and there were churches whose spires overshadowed the saloons and dance halls. The cavalry band occasionally came into town to give concerts, a circulat-

ing library provided books, and the Young Men's Literary Society was trying to bring culture to people not accustomed to discussing the niceties of the newest novel.

The arrival of the railroad was a gala occasion in Tucson. The first train to steam its way into town on March 20, 1880, was greeted by a thirty-eight-gun salute by troopers from Fort Lowell and by music by the cavalry band. Charles Crocker was on hand to drive the last spike—which appropriately was of silver from the Tough Nut mine at nearby Tombstone; officials at the Southern Pacific were delighted with the discovery of silver at Tombstone in 1878 and the rapid growth of this town, for its 12,000 residents would need supplies and the bullion would have to be transported out of the territory on Southern Pacific trains.

After the formal festivities had concluded, the dignitaries adjourned to the comfort of Charles Brown's saloon. There the mayor and other leaders of Tucson, between beers, decided they should

184

Tucson, looking east from the court house, about the time
of the arrival of the railroad. *Courtesy Arizona Historical Society.*

spread the happy news of the arrival of the railroad in their town
to officials across the United States. Mayor Robert Leatherwood
therefore sent telegrams to the president and vice president of the
United States, to leaders in Congress, to the governor of Arizona,
and to the mayors of such cities as New York, Chicago, San Francisco, Los Angeles, Yuma, and even to Phoenix, which was Tuc
son's bitter rival for dominance in Arizona. Finally the question
was raised if any important figure had been omitted, and someone
suggested the Pope. However, it appeared that no one present
knew where the Pope lived, so a messenger was sent to Pete Kitch-
en's ranch south of town; his wife was Mexican and Catholic, and
she supplied the information that the Pope resided in Rome, Italy.

The telegram then was drafted: "The Pope, Rome, Italy. The
Mayor of Tucson begs the honor of reminding His Holiness that
this ancient and honorable pueblo was founded by the Spaniards
under the sanction of the Church more than three centuries ago

185

and to inform your Holiness that a railroad from San Francisco, California, now connects us with the Christian world. Asking your benediction."

One by one the telegrams arrived during the course of the evening, and as each was brought to Charles Brown's saloon Mayor Bob Leatherwood would read it to the throng—to cheers and yet more drinks. Finally came one bearing the Pope's name. Leatherwood read it aloud, but not to cheers: "Am glad the railroad has reached Tucson, but where the H—— is Tucson?"[2]

Sober at last from their celebration, the work crews turned their attention to pushing the track on to the east toward El Paso. On this stretch of the work the army furnished a military escort to protect the laborers from attacks by roving bands of Apaches. Twenty miles east of Tucson came the depot named Vail for the ranch in the area; then down they dropped to the San Pedro River where the town of Benson grew. Six ten-degree curves were necessary to get the train over this river crossing, but the forty miles from Tucson had been laid rapidly; the first train reached Benson on June 22, 1880.

Across the San Pedro the track climbed sharply through a stand of mountains, crossed over into the Sulphur Springs Valley, and moved across it to the town of Willcox. Then, emerging from this fertile valley, it marched toward New Mexico not quite on the route of the old Butterfield Route; instead it went ten miles north of Fort Bowie to a point designated as "Bowie." This was the heart of the Chiricahua Apache country, but the work proceeded rapidly.

Breaking into New Mexico, the track-layers found their work much easier. This section of the Gila Trail was flat desert country, and they raced into Lordsburg on October 18, 1880, and Deming on December 15. At Las Cruces (formerly known as Mesilla), the track turned to parallel the Rio Grande to El Paso, which was reached on May 19, 1881. The men had been pushed hard across this region because Jay Gould had his Texas and Pacific tracks moving rapidly across western Texas at this time.

The celebration at El Paso over the arrival of the first train was as lavish as the town could afford. The town was little more

Depot of the Southern Pacific in Tucson (about 1890).
Courtesy Arizona Historical Society.

than a collection of shacks baked to a dusty brown by a hot sun. But it had changed its name from Franklin to El Paso when the little Mexican town across the river had abandoned the old designation in favor of Juarez. The American town numbered only seven hundred inhabitants. A journey down the main—unpaved—street of the city was pleasant, however, for it was lined by heavy, plastered adobe columns and arches which created a shaded portico to keep citizens out of the sun. Lumber was a scarce commodity, and thus everything was built of adobe. With the arrival of the railroad, however, lumber was brought in quantity, and within a year the population had doubled and buildings became more American in appearance. Other big city luxuries arrived soon after the railroad: indoor plumbing, electric lights, piped gas, and even banking facilities. In fact, the arrival of the railroad proved such a boon that some businesses opened in tents until new structures could be erected, this in a city where the streets turned into rivers of mud when it rained.

By the agreement made earlier between Huntington and Gould, the Southern Pacific was supposed to halt at El Paso, there to be joined by the Texas and Pacific. Moreover, the Southern Pacific had charters only from the legislatures of New Mexico and Arizona, but none in Texas. Yet the Big Four of the Southern Pacific did not want to be halted in their drive to the Gulf of Mexico by having to deal with Jay Gould for right of way. The Texas and Pacific was moving westward across Texas, but in no great hurry, for Gould thought his agreement with Huntington guaranteed his control of rails east of El Paso.

But the laying of track by Southern Pacific crews did not halt at El Paso. It continued straight on to the east across Texas. A stunned Jay Gould questioned this only to learn that the Big Four in 1880 had purchased a large interest in an obscure Texas railroad called the Galveston, Harrisburg and San Antonio. This line, founded by Tom Peirce, ran between the cities carried in its title, and under the new ownership began building westward from San Antonio in 1881. When asked the destination of these rails, Peirce would answer only that they were bound "somewhere." That somewhere turned out to be El Paso. And at El Paso building eastward were Southern Pacific crews, running tracks to join with the Galveston, Harrisburg and San Antonio.

The country immediately east of El Paso was rugged and mountainous. In fact, there was only one pass through these mountains; this was the one at Sierra Blanca 90 miles from El Paso. Naturally both the Southern Pacific and the Texas and Pacific wanted to reach this pass first and gain control of it. Charles Crocker sent his veteran builder, J. H. Strobridge, to join with William Hood and push track rapidly through the pass. At the same time the track which Peirce had been laying west from San Antonio to "somewhere" arrived at Del Rio on the Mexican border, thus opening the way for freighting into that country; from Del Rio it was rushed toward the town of Marathon 197 miles away and then on toward the pass at Sierra Blanca. Hood worked out the route of construction for the Galveston, Harrisburg and San Antonio, while Huntington ordered the men and material sent to Peirce. Suddenly laying track through southwest Texas were Chinese laborers and Irish rail jugglers who had only months before been working in the snows of the mighty Sierra. Strobridge offered a cash bonus to all men who would stay with the job until it was completed.

Beyond Del Rio the task proved difficult, for track was moving across limestone cliffs bordering the Rio Grande. But ever westward moved the Galveston, Houston and San Antonio, reaching the Pecos and crossing it in 1882 by means of a bridge that was a marvel of engineering, a tunnel was driven through a mountain to provide the take-off point for the bridge, and then another tunnel made the ascent on the far side of the stream. Just to the west of this second tunnel, the work crews of the Galveston, Houston and San Antonio met the work crews of the Southern Pacific at 2:00 p.m. on January 12, 1883. Tom Peirce was on hand to drive the last spike.

Jay Gould had lost the race. His Texas and Pacific tracklayers reached Sierra Blanca on January 1, 1882, and tied into the Southern Pacific's tracks, but he could move freight west of that point only by paying tribute to the Big Four of Southwestern rail-

189

roading. However, Gould still came out well. From the state of Texas alone he received 5,167,000 acres of land as a bonus for the track he had laid. Huntington and the Southern Pacific did not fare so well. Congress refused to endorse the transfer of the land bonus given in the original charter to the Texas and Pacific, and thus the Southern Pacific did not get federal subsidies for the work it had done in Arizona and New Mexico. Yet the Southern Pacific had protected its monopoly on railroading to California, and it had gained transcontinental status by completing its track from the Pacific Coast to the Gulf of Mexico. And another bit of track-laying from Galveston eastward soon opened traffic to New Orleans, so that the Sunset Route was advertised and opened to service on February 5, 1883. This 2069-mile journey brought trains speeding across the Southwest in the same number of days that previously had been months for wagons and weeks for stage-coaches.[3]

The coming of the railroad to the Gila Trail brought a new breed of hero to young boys living near the tracks. Previously they had worshipped the teamsters who drove wagons, cracking their whips and cursing so loudly. Then had come the day of the stage driver, that proud man who sat atop his seat and drove six mules with such ease. Now it was the engineer to whom young boys gave their loyalty and whose seat they aspired some day to fill. Laying awake in their beds at night, they could hear in the distance the whistle of the train and dream of driving such a mighty engine someday; they could stand at the depot and watch the monster rush in, blowing steam for breath and carrying with it the smell of adventure and of distant lands. The engineer was more a legendary figure to lads who had never been far from home than ever was a knight of old; his overalls and his denim cap might not shine like metal, but he was a man in command of a steam engine that rolled across the land—and that was enough.

The man in charge of the freight depot in each town dotting the tracks was not so glamorous, but he became an important figure in the economic life of each village. He superintended the unloading of the freight cars dropped at his siding, and he was the one to

Blasting the right of way for the railroad. *From Harper's Weekly.*

Typical depot during the days of early railroading. *From Harper's Weekly.*

whom every merchant went to get his consignment of goods. Farmers had to discuss with him the number of railroad cars they needed to move their crops to market, and ranchers arranged shipping dates for moving their cattle to the slaughter houses on the West Coast or in the Midwest. Even the mail came by train, and the postmaster brought outgoing letters and packages to the depot to be sent out, and there he picked up the sacks containing mail for the citizens served at this post office. Also, the civilian telegraph lines that paralleled the railroad tracks were manned usually in offices at local depots.

Thus the local railroad depot of the Southern Pacific became the economic center of almost every town along the Gila Trail. Mail, freight, and passengers met there, as did messages of such importance that they came over the telegraph. Moreover, these depots were social gathering places, their benches the spot where local gossip was exchanged and where old men came to while away long sunny afternoons. Small children gathered near the depot to watch the Sunset Limited pass through at incredible speed, just as they came to see what the local freight train would deliver. In short, the local depot became the center of town, the one place where men confined to an isolated life could meet with the outside world. It provided what Southwesterners had been demanding since the days of the gold rush—rapid, efficient transportation for people, for freight, and for communication.

The result of the opening of the railroad was immediately felt, not only in the new towns that grew up along the way but in the older cities. Fort Worth, which had been a sleepy village of only 1600 people in 1873, boomed to 30,000 residents by 1888. El Paso likewise grew, as did Tucson and Yuma. Where once this region had been seen only by the most hardy men, it now was visited by tourists who came through on the Pacific Express to marvel at how foreign, how un-American, the region seemed. At the same time the railroad made the region more American, for over it came the machinery for ice-making plants at every town of any size; along it were built restaurants that served more traditional food than beans and chili. Clean hotels were erected to cater to the

192

tenderfoot and the tourist who did not want to sleep on the crude bed of the pioneer. Suddenly there everywhere was hustle and bustle, new economic activity, new growth.

El Paso became an example of this growth. In 1885 *Harper's Magazine* carried an article about the town that stated: "Where, only a few months before, the complaining 'tenderfoot' was cursing the miserable fare of the country, the tourist breakfasts, dines, and sups leisurely at a succession of cheerful railway hotels. . . . Everywhere are signs of an awakened, stirring line, which has changed the country as in the twinkling of an eye." Indeed it had, for by the end of the decade of the 1880s, El Paso had grown to 10,000 people—with more arriving every day.

These changes caused many old-timers in the region to complain about the softness of the new life. They said that the influx of people was ruining the region, that they felt crowded, that the old days were better. Better or worse, however, the railroad and the telegraph had revolutionized life in the Southwest. Where once transportation had been by stage coach, freight wagon, or even pack mule, where letters had moved at four or five miles an hour to their destination, and where goods had to be made locally or else done without, they now had civilization coming to them over rails of steel. Life may or may not have been better in the old days, but it never again would be the same.

9

Aftermath

In a book of extraordinary perception, *The Tyranny of Distance,* Geoffrey Blainey in 1964 sought to explain Australian failure to develop rapidly to its paucity of major rivers which could have opened the interior of the continent and served as arteries of transportation and communication. In developing his thesis, he contrasted the slow settlement of the Outback, as the arid interior of Australia is known, to the rapid expansion of settlers into the interior of the United States.

Blainey was correct in this assessment—for the eastern part of the United States. The first settlers there did find numerous rivers of sufficient size to serve as highways, carrying first the canoes and flatboats of the pioneers and then the steamboats of a later era. However, as the descendants of those early settlers moved into the American Southwest, they found no such rivers, and development slowed to a snail's pace. Only one river in the Southwest was of sufficient width and depth to be an artery of commerce: the Colorado River; but that stream flowed north to south for the length of Arizona's western border, and then turned eastward through the Grand Canyon into the rugged Four-Corners country (where Utah, Colorado, Arizona, and New Mexico join) and the mountains of western Colorado. For most of its journey the Colorado thus flowed through land of spectacular scenic but little economic value.

Without major rivers to navigate, the early American pilgrims to view the Southwest looked upon it as a land of little value, a region to be crossed as rapidly as possible to get to the gold fields or the farming lands of California. They, as the Spaniards before them, were unable to settle the land in any numbers or to turn it to productive use, and it remained largely the homeland of native Americans. Arizona and New Mexico, along with the desert por-

Old Modoc Stage, used in the early Eighties, at Tombstone, Ariz.

Above.
A Modoc stage used in the
early 1880s in southern Arizona.
Courtesy Arizona Historical Society.

Left.
William S. Oury, mayor
of Tucson, when the railroad arrived.
Courtesy Arizona Historical Society.

tion of southern California, became most unusual American possessions: at once old in terms of colonial settlement, in some instances pre-dating the founding of Jamestown and Plymouth Bay, but yet new in terms of development. As late as 1900 the populations of Arizona and New Mexico were so small that they had not attained statehood.

However, the pattern of settlement of the Southwest—Americans pushing west to the barrier of the desert and then jumping across to the Pacific Coast—coupled with the gold rush to California forced the political leaders of the day to search for new methods of transportation to carry the mail and people. Californians were asking—in fact, demanding—that they be linked more closely with the Union as the decade of the 1850s moved forward. Inasmuch as the old method of transportation by water was unusable and because the normal pattern of settlement had been disrupted to the point that regular roads had not developed, the president and Congress were forced to pioneer themselves. Hence President James K. Polk sent orders for General Stephen Watts Kearny to have part of his troops open a wagon road from Santa Fe to California; hence Congress decreed that the postmaster-general should negotiate a contract to subsidize a transcontinental mail route.

The road that was opened in this process, Cooke's Wagon Road, renamed the Gila Trail, became like a river in its importance in Southwestern history. Over it flowed people, the mail, and goods, but the vehicles were wagons and stagecoaches, not keelboats and steamboats (ironically the wagon used was known as a "schooner," although it did have the word "prairie" prefixed to it). And there were landing points along this trail just as there were along the rivers, way-stations where stagecoach passengers could rest and get meals, small towns with freight depots and stock pens.

By the time the Gila Trail was developing, the railroad was technologically feasible, but political considerations slowed its building across this desert wasteland. And again it was a case of "the tyranny of distance," for had the Southwest been settled in the normal pattern there would have been sufficient people in the region to make the building of a railroad financially rewarding for

196

private enterprise; such had been the case in the East where no federal subsidies of any magnitude had been necessary. Across the Southwest, however, there were so few people that the project was financially impossible for private enterprise, and a federal subsidy was necessary. The end result was the discussion of the project in Congress, where it became embroiled in sectional hatreds that postponed it until after the Civil War became a reality. Without this "tyranny of distance," the Southwest thus would have been opened a decade, and possibly two, earlier than it was.

The opening of the railroad was a milestone of sorts, for with it came ready access to the outside world. For the first time in its history the people were assured of rapid transportation of people and goods and mail, while the arrival of a concomitant of the railroad, the telegraph, meant that Southwesterners also had instant access to quick communication. Through the telegraph they received the latest market information, along with political and social news that made them feel part of the United States and, to a lesser extent, the world at large. Once the "iron horse" arrived, the provincialism of the Southwest had been cracked.

A few men alive at that time realized the significance of this step. When Charles Crocker came to Tucson in March 1880 to participate in the ceremonies celebrating the arrival of the railroad in that city, he listened to many speeches. Some were given by local politicians hopeful of gaining national office, while others were masterpieces of local pride. But there was one speech not written on the wind of political ambition that day. It came from the mayor of Tucson at that time, William S. Oury, a man who virtually had lived the history of the Gila Trail and who could realize the significance of what was transpiring that March day.

Almost half a century before Oury had been the last man out of the Alamo; he had been chosen to carry the final message from the beseiged fort because at age fifteen he was the youngest man there. He had fought at San Jacinto under General Sam Houston to help Texas achieve its independence. Later he had been a Texas Ranger, then had moved west across the Gila Trail to settle at Tucson. There he had ranched and had fought as a Confederate in the Civil War. His brother Granville had served as Arizona's representative in the Confederate congress at Richmond. After that war, William S. Oury had gone into business in Tucson and had been active in local politics, just as he had fought to bring the railroad to the region.

"Our mission is ended today," he said to the assembled guests at the celebration on March 20, referring to old-timers such as himself. "Here then arises the question, what are you to do with us? The enterprise of such men as now surround me has penetrated every corner of our broad land, and we now have no frontier to which the pioneer may flee to avoid the tramp of civilized progress. . . ." Oury concluded his speech that day by noting that he and most other early settlers of the region were growing older, or, as he put it, "The weight of years has fallen upon us." He called on the younger men in his audience to continue to fight for progress, especially in taking from the earth the precious metals for which the region was famous. "However," he cautioned them, "in the whirl of excitement incident to the race after the treasure embedded in our mountain ranges, our last request is that you kindly avoid trampling into the dust the few remaining monuments of the first American settlements."[1]

Here he could easily have been speaking about the area along the entire Gila Trail, not just for Arizona. Somehow in the years that followed the monuments to early settlement did not die, and the trail itself continued to be used. Wagons and buggies would follow in its ruts, although few men any longer drove them the entire distance of the trail. Then shortly after the turn of the twentieth century came yet a new mode of transportation, the wheezing and coughing and noisy thing at first regarded as little more than a toy, the automobile. Advocates of this conveyance were dedicated, however, and they banded together into associations to promote both their mode of travel and good roads over which to drive. In 1908 the Automobile Club of Southern California conceived the idea of a road race from Los Angeles to Phoenix as a means of promoting good roads; residents of Phoenix were delighted to participate, for the race ended during the week of the territorial (after 1912 the state) fair. Some years the "Cactus Derby," as this race was labeled, went from Los Angeles to San Diego to Yuma to

198

Phoenix; other years it ran from Los Angeles to Needles, California, to Prescott, Arizona, to Phoenix, but always it generated excitement and promoted paved roads.[2] Other promoters sponsored motorcycle races from El Paso to Phoenix, most of the route going over the Gila Trail.

Gradually such promotion resulted in the paving of the trail with asphalt—"US 80" it was named. Still this paving was not without great difficulty, for the sandy desert of southern California, which had been so tiring on men and animals in the days of wagons and stagecoaches, resisted pavement as it had fought the vehicles of an earlier age. The first hard-surfaced road across this stretch of desert in the twentieth century consisted of planks held together by ropes. Modern engineering finally solved the problem, however, and it, like the rest of the Gila Trail, was crossed by a two-lane, asphalt road. Then with the federal Highway Act of 1956 it became part of the superhighway system so that today it is known as Interstate 8 from San Diego to Casa Grande, Arizona, and from there eastward to El Paso it is Interstate 10.

The great-grandchildren of Forty-Niners who cross the Southwest do so in air-conditioned automobiles at speeds of some seventy miles per hour. Traveling at this rate it is easy for the modern pilgrim to begin to believe there is a uniformity to the geography of the United States, for much of what he sees is a blur and a haze. Also, the traveler usually is not watching the scenery closely; rather he is searching for signs informing him about service stations, restaurants, and motels. He does not really see the towns and villages along the way, just an occasional major city where he stops briefly for gasoline or to spend the night. Without really straining this pilgrim can make three hundred to four hundred miles in a day—or even five hundred miles if he pushes hard between an early breakfast and a late dinner.

About all the average tourist, who whips across the paved-over remains of the Gila Trail, notes is that the towns have strange names: San Diego, El Centro, Yuma, Gila Bend, Casa Grande, Tucson, Benson, Willcox, Lordsburg, Deming, Las Cruces, El Paso. And he decides, from the vantage point of his air-conditioned automobile, that the region is harsh and inhospitable, a land of

The plank road west of Yuma.
Atop the rise on the left are workmen constructing the paved highway.
Courtesy Arizona Historical Society.

cactus, sagebrush, and tumbleweeds and of too much heat and too little rain. Yet the really curious visitor who looks closer at the land of the Gila Trail will find the region incredibly rich even without traveling at the five-mile-per-hour pace of the rider of the Butterfield stage.

First, the land is rich in history. Its Indians have a long and proud history, one that reveals levels of civilization equal, if not superior, to that of other parts of the United States. It is a land settled by European colonists long before Jamestown and Plymouth Bay were visited by Englishmen. Spaniards first visited the region some three-quarters of a century before those noteworthy events, and the names of those bold conquistadors still ring with romance: Alvar Nuñez Cabeza de Vaca, Estebanico the Black, Fray Marcos de Niza, Francisco Vásquez de Coronado, Juan de Oñate. Successively the land was under the flags of Spain and Mexico and even the Bear Flag of the short-lived Republic of California—before seeing the Stars and Stripes and individual state flags. This was the land of the explorer, the bearded mountain man in search of beaver pelts, the prospector, the cowhand, the sodbuster, the soldier, the stage-driver, the bullwhacker, the telegrapher, and the railroader.

These are the men who pioneered the economy of the region, just as they are the ones who pushed the Southwest from a land of trails known only to Indians to that of wagon and stage roads, to gravel-surfaced roads, to paved two-lane ribbons of asphalt, to the four-lane concrete freeways of today. They are the people who pioneered the movement of passengers, freight, and the mail by means of wagons, stagecoaches, railroads, automobiles, and finally airplanes.

The land of the Gila Trail is rich in geography, incredibly blessed with a vivid landscape that varies from mountains to valleys, from lakes to deserts, from towering pines to thorny cacti, from lush vegetation to rolling and barren sand dunes. It ranges from below sea level in the Imperial Desert of Southern California to many thousands of feet high in mountains whose summits know snow nine to ten months of the year. It has summer resort country and widely known attractions for winter visitors; sand buggies race within fifty miles of ski facilities—and both operate simultaneously.

Finally, the Gila Trail region is rich in people, including Indians, Latin Americans, blacks, Orientals, and Anglo-Americans. Just as its geography ranges from the pleasant and mild to the harsh and inhospitable, so its people vary from good to bad and in between. Here have been performed deeds of daring, of dishonor, of valor, and of dishonesty.

And just as the region changed in the years that William S. Oury knew it, so it has changed in the decades that have passed since 1880. Today the land of the Gila Trail is one of cities, of urbanized communities surrounded by farms that grow everything, of ranches featuring the best known breeds of cattle, along with feed lots and packing plants. And it is a region that has ecological problems, such as smog, urban blight, and pollution.

Yes, the old Southwest is changed, utterly and entirely. But it is change built upon the past. There are still echoes of the region that was—echoes in the vast, open spaces between the cities, and echoes in the architecture, place-names, food, dress, even the patterns of speech and thought in the metropolitan areas. The winds of ten thousand dust devils have not blown away the tradition of hospitality and generosity, of courage and fortitude, and of informality and openness. These traits of a unique past linger to provide inspiration to the descendants of young lads who once worshipped stage-drivers and then locomotive engineers.

The youngsters of today turn their eyes toward the sky to find their heroes, toward jet airline pilots who travel the entirety of the Gila Trail in less than two hours—about the length of time it took a teamster to round up his mules or oxen and get them hitched. Or today's young people look even farther into the sky to the spacemen who have journeyed to the moon to find their heroes. But as they gaze skyward, these youngsters should realize that the dust about their feet once was swirled by the wheels of stage-coaches and freight wagons. They should know that the spark of the telegraph and the lonesome whistle of a freight train at midnight are as much a part of the Southwest as is the asphalt and concrete of a superhighway. These are what made possible both the present and the future.

Notes

Chapter 1

1. Details of this "fight" are in Philip St. George Cooke, "Journal of the March of the Mormon Battalion of Infantry Volunteers under the Command of Lieut. Col. P. St. Geo. Cooke . . . ," *Senate Document 2*, 30 Cong., Special Session, 93-94; also published in Ralph P. Bieber and Averam B. Bender (eds.), *Exploring Southwestern Trails* (in Southwest Historical Series, Vol. VII, Glendale, California, 1938). Hereafter cited as Cooke, "Mormon Battalion Journal." For additional details, see Cooke, *The Conquest of New Mexico and California in 1846-1848* (New York, 1878, and reprint), 147-50. In his account of this march, Cooke paused between accounts of the approaching battle at Tucson to record his impressions about the geography of the region.

2. See Frank A. Golder, Thomas A. Bailey, and J. Lyman Smith, *The March of the Mormon Battalion* (New York, 1928), 195-96; Cooke, "Mormon Battalion Journal," 91-94; and Cooke, "Report on the March of the Mormon Battalion, February 5, 1847," *House Document 41*, 30 Cong., 1 Sess., 556-57.

3. For a description of life in Tucson at this time, see Odie B. Faulk and Sidney B. Brinckerhoff, "Soldiering at the End of the World," *The American West*, III (summer 1966), 28-37.

4. Cooke, *The Conquest of New Mexico and California*, 152-53.

5. There are many good books giving a general history of the Apaches. These include Will C. Barnes, *Apaches and Longhorns* (Los Angeles, 1941); Gordon Baldwin, *The Warrior Apaches* (Tucson, 1966); Grenville Goodwin, *The Social Organization of the Western Apache Indians* (New York, 1938); Morris E. Opler, *An Apache Life-Way* (Chicago, 1941); and Edward H. Spicer, *Cycles of Conquest* (Tucson, 1962).

6. For the story of this effort, see Herbert E. Bolton, *Anza's California Expeditions* (5 vols.; Berkeley, 1930); and Elliott Coues (trans. and ed.), *On the Trail of a Spanish Pioneer: The Diary and Itinerary of Francisco Garcés . . .* (2 vols.; New York, 1900).

7. See Lowell J. Bean and William M. Mason, *Diaries and Accounts of the Romero Expeditions in Arizona and California* (Palm Springs, California, 1962).

8. For the background causes of this conflict, see Seymour V. Connor and Odie B. Faulk, *North America Divided: The Mexican War, 1846-1848* (New York, 1971), 3-32.

9. For a good biography of Stephen W. Kearny, see D. L. Clarke, *Stephen Watts Kearny: Soldier of the West* (Norman, 1961).

10. Cooke, *Conquest of New Mexico and California,* 146; Cooke, "Mormon Battalion Journal," 83.

11. Henry W. Bigler, "Extracts from the Journal of Henry W. Bigler," *Utah Historical Quarterly,* V (1933), 46; and Nathaniel V. Jones, "Journal of Nathaniel V. Jones, with the Mormon Battalion," *Utah Historical Quarterly,* IV (1931), 7.

12. Daniel Tyler, *Concise History of the Mormon Battalion in the Mexican War* (Salt Lake City, 1881, and reprint), 214-15.

13. Cooke, "Mormon Battalion Journal," 86-87.

14. Brigham H. Roberts, *The Mormon Battalion: Its History and Achievements* (Salt Lake City, 1919), 85.

15. Kearny, after his arrival in California, faced hostilities from a Mexican counter-revolution; this rumor probably concerned the Battle of San Pascual. See Connor and Faulk, *North America Divided,* 92-93.

16. Cooke, "Mormon Battalion Journal," 180-196. For an excellent biography of Cooke, see Otis E. Young, Jr., *The West of Philip St. George Cooke, 1809-1895* (Glendale, California, 1955).

Chapter 2

1. "Treaty of Peace, Friendship, Limits and Settlement between the United States of America and the Mexican Republic, concluded at Guadalupe Hidalgo, on the 2d Day of February, in the year 1848," in William M. Malloy (comp.), *Treaties, Conventions, International Acts, Protocols and Agreements Between the United States of America and Other Powers, 1776-1909* (2 vols.; Washington, D.C., 1910), I, 1109-13; see also George P. Hammond (ed.), *The Treaty of Guadalupe Hidalgo* (Berkeley, 1949), for an excellent study of this treaty.

2. Cave J. Couts, *From San Diego to the Colorado in 1849: the Journal and Maps of Cave J. Couts,* edited by William McPherson (Los Angeles, 1932), 48-49. Whipple also kept an account; see "Report of the Secretary of War," January 31, 1851, *Senate Executive Document 19,* 31 Cong., 2 Sess.; reprinted as A. W. Whipple, *The Whipple Report,* edited by E. I. Edwards (Los Angeles, 1961).

3. D. C. Goddard, Secretary of the Interior *ad interim,* to J. R. Bartlett, New York, August 1, 1850, in *Senate Executive Document 119,* 32 Cong., 1 Sess.; hereafter cited as *SED 119.* For details of Bartlett's life, see

Robert V. Hine, *Bartlett's West: Drawing the Mexican Boundary* (New Haven, 1968).

4. See John C. Cremony, *Life Among the Apaches* (San Francisco, 1868, and reprint), 18-19.

5. Bartlett, *Personal Narrative of Exploration and Incidents* . . . (2 vols.; New York, 1854, and reprint), I, 152; and "Report of the Secretary of the Interior, Communicating . . . a Copy of the Charges Preferred against the Present Commissioner Appointed to Run and Mark the Boundary Line . . . ," *Senate Executive Document 60*, 32 Cong., 1 Sess., 52-53.

6. "A complaint against the commissary on account of the insufficiency and inferiority of provisions," *SED 119*, 42-43, as well as other correspondence in *SED 119*, 43-46, 49-50, 53-55; and Carlysle Graham Raht, *The Romance of Davis Mountains and Big Bend Country* (Odessa, Texas, 1963), 105-12.

7. Hammond (ed.), *Treaty of Guadalupe Hidalgo*, 69-70.

8. Correspondence in *SED 119*, 37-38, 386-91; J. Fred Rippy, *The United States and Mexico* (New York, 1931), 109-10; and Humberto Escoto Ochoa, *Integración y Desintegración de Nuestra Frontera Norte* (Mexico City, 1949), 126.

9. *SED 119*, 145-49, 213-14, 243-46, 279-84; Bartlett, *Personal Narrative*, I, 376; and "Report of A. B. Gray, with a map in relation to the Mexican Boundary," *Senate Executive Document 55*, 33 Cong., 2 Sess., 4, 13, 27-28.

10. What would become Fort Yuma was first established by Lieutenant Cave J. Couts and his troops of the 1st Dragoons on October 2, 1849; the post was named Camp Calhoun in honor of John Calhoun. There it remained until December 1, 1850, when it was moved by Major Samuel P. Heintzelman to a point just below the ferry crossing, at which time it was designated Camp Independence. Later it would be abandoned, then reestablished at Fort Yuma. For a history of the post, see Ray Brandes, *Frontier Military Posts of Arizona* (Globe, Ariz., 1960), 81-86.

11. "The Boundary Line: Trials and Adventures of the Surveyors as Described by General Frank Wheaton," Tucson *Arizona Daily Citizen*, July 27, 1895.

12. This was his *Personal Narrative*.

13. *SED 119*, 118-19; and "Report of the Committee on Foreign Relations . . . in relation to fixing the initial point in the boundary line between the United States and Mexico . . . August 20, 1852," *Senate Report 345*, 32 Cong., 1 Sess., 4-5.

14. Bartlett, *Personal Narrative*, II, 514-16.

15. The hearings against Bartlett constitute *SED 119*. See also *Senate Report 345*, as well as various speeches in the *Congressional Globe*. The appropriations act for 1852-53 is in the *Congressional Globe*, XXIV, part 3, p. xviii.

16. Bartlett, *Personal Narrative,* II, 514-16.

17. See *House Report 81,* 33 Cong., 1 Sess., 1-2; and Calvin Horn, *New Mexico's Troubled Years* (Albuquerque, 1963), 47.

18. See *House Report 81,* 33 Cong., 1 Sess., 1-2; Ochoa, *Integración y Desintegración,* 130-31; Francisco R. Almada, "Governadores del Estado: Gral. D. Ángel Trias," *Boletín de la Sociedad Chihuahuense de Estudios Historicos,* III (July and August 1941), 172-88; and Paul Neff Garber, *The Gadsden Treaty* (Gloucester, Mass., 1959), 71.

19. Wilfrid H. Callcott, *Santa Anna: The Story of an Enigma Who Once Was Mexico* (Norman, 1936), 278-85; and Rippy, *The United States and Mexico,* 127.

20. Malloy, *Treaties,* 1113.

21. These instructions are in David H. Miller (ed.), *Treaties and Other International Acts of the United States of America* (8 vols.; Washington, D.C., 1942-48), VI, 342-47. See also Garber, *The Gadsden Treaty,* 83-85, and Rippy, *The United States and Mexico,* 128.

22. This treaty is in Miller, *Treaties,* VI, 318-22.

23. In this effort he failed by drawing the boundary about ten miles too far north to include all Cooke's road.

24. Owing to the twists and turns of the Colorado, this point is actually twenty-eight miles below the junction of the Gila and Colorado rivers; for details of this treaty's fate in the United States Senate, see Ochoa, *Integración and Desintegración,* 135; Rippy, *The United States and Mexico,* 151-52; William R. Matthews, "An Answer to a Century-Old Question," Tucson *Arizona Daily Star,* September 15, 1965, Section F, p. 10; and Luis G. Zorrilla, *Historia de las Relaciones entre Mexico y Los Estados Unidos de America, 1800-1958* (2 vols.; Mexico City, 1965-66), I, 351-54.

25. For details of these events, see Emory, "Report of the United States and Mexican Boundary Commission," *Senate Executive Document 108,* 34 Cong., 1 Sess. (3 vols. in 2).

Chapter 3

1. The details of the Duval party's trek are contained in Benjamin Butler Harris, *The Gila Trail: The Texas Argonauts and the California Gold Rush,* edited by Richard H. Dillon (Norman, 1960).

2. This is exactly what happened to Sutter. For details, see Richard Dillon, *Fool's Gold: The Decline and Fall of Captain John Sutter of California* (New York, 1967), and James P. Zollinger, *Sutter: The Man and His Empire* (New York, 1939).

3. Examples of such editorials and advertisements can be found in the major newspapers for each of the cities involved during the years 1849-52.

4. A copy of the passport obtained by Captain Duval from Mexican authorities at El Paso can be found in Sidney Brinckerhoff, "Passport to Mexico," *The Journal of Arizona History*, VIII (spring 1967), 54-59.

5. Details of the Neighbors-Ford expedition can be found in John Salmon Ford, Memoirs (transcript, 7 vols.; Archives, University of Texas Library), III, 503ff.; C. L. Greenwood (ed.), "Opening Routes to El Paso, 1849," *Southwestern Historical Quarterly*, XLVIII (October 1944), 262-74; Kenneth F. Neighbours (ed.), "The Report of the Expedition of Major Robert S. Neighbors to El Paso in 1849," *Southwestern Historical Quarterly*, LX (April 1957), 527-32; and Mabelle E. Martin, "California Emigrant Roads Through Texas," *Southwestern Historical Quarterly*, XXVIII (April 1925), 287-301.

6. "Report of Captain R. B. Marcy," contained in "Report of the Secretary of War," *Senate Executive Document 64*, 31 Cong., 1 Sess. See also Grant Foreman (ed.), *Marcy and the Gold Seekers* (Norman, 1937), and W. Eugene Hollon, *Beyond the Cross Timbers: The Travels of Randolph B. Marcy, 1812-1887* (Norman, 1955).

7. Charles Pancoast, *A Quaker Forty-Niner: The Adventures of Charles Edward Pancoast on the American Frontier*, edited by Anna P. Hannum (Philadelphia, 1930), 249-50. For a good secondary account of travelers on this trail, see Ferol Egan, *The El Dorado Trail: The Story of the Gold Rush Routes Across Mexico* (New York, 1970).

8. The entire story of these sisters can be found in R. B. Stratton, *Captivity of the Oatman Girls* (New York, 1859, and reprint).

9. Cave J. Couts, *From San Diego to the Colorado in 1849: The Journal and Maps of Cave J. Couts*, edited by William McPherson (Los Angeles, 1932), 48.

10. *Ibid.*, 48-49.

11. Ralph A. Smith, "The Scalp Hunter in the Borderlands," *Arizona and the West*, VI (spring 1964), 5-22; and Ralph A. Smith, "Apache 'Ranching' Below the Gila, 1841-1845," *Arizoniana*, III (winter 1962), 1-17.

12. James G. Bell, "A Log of the Texas-California Cattle Trail," edited by J. Evetts Haley, *Southwestern Historical Quarterly*, XXXV and XXXVI (January, April, and July 1932), 208-37, 290-316, 47-66.

13. For a picture of life in the gold fields, see Chapter I in Robert G. Ferris (ed.), *Prospector, Cowhand, and Sodbuster: Historic Places Associated with the Mining, Ranching, and Farming Frontiers in the Trans-Mississippi West* (Washington, D.C., 1967), 3-81.

Chapter 4

1. See "Reports of Explorations and Surveys," *Senate Executive Document 78*, 33 Cong., 2 Sess. These ten volumes generally are referred to as the *Pacific Railroad Reports*.

2. L. R. Bailey (ed.), *The A. B. Gray Report* (Los Angeles, 1963).

3. John C. Duval, *The Adventures of Big-Foot Wallace* (Lincoln, 1935, 1966).

4. A brief history of this organization can be found in Roscoe P. Conkling and Margaret B. Conkling, *The Butterfield Overland Mail, 1857-1869* (3 vols.; Glendale, 1947), I, 92-100.

5. "Postmaster-General's Report," *Senate Executive Document 13,* 36 Cong., 1 Sess., Vol. III, 141.

6. Quoted, *ibid.,* I, 135-36. Chapter I in this book contains a biographical sketch of Butterfield. For a checklist of books relating to the Butterfield effort, see William Tallack, *The California Overland Express* (Los Angeles, 1935); this work has an introduction by Carl I. Wheat, and after Tallack's account is a checklist of titles compiled by J. Gregg Layne.

7. Waterman L. Ormsby, *The Butterfield Overland Mail,* edited by Lyle H. Wright and Josephine M. Bynum (San Marino, Cal., 1968), 32. These articles originally appeared in the New York *Herald,* and can also be found in W. B. Lang, *The First Overland Mail, Butterfield Trail* (Washington, D.C., 1940).

8. *Ibid.,* 40. See also Thomas E. Farish, *History of Arizona* (8 vols.; Phoenix, 1915), II, 1-10.

9. Ormsby, *The Butterfield Overland Mail,* 129.

10. W. Eugene Hollon, "Great Days of the Overland Stage," *American Heritage,* VIII (June 1957), 27-31, 101.

11. For details of the "Bascom Affair," as this tragic event is known, see Robert M. Utley, "The Bascom Affair: A Reconstruction," *Arizona and the West,* III (spring 1961), 59-68; and B. Sacks, "New Evidence on the Bascom Affair," *Arizona and the West,* IV (autumn 1962), 261-78.

Chapter 5

1. *Congressional Globe,* XXV (1855-56), 1297-99.

2. *Ibid.,* XXVI (1856-57), 611-12. See also *U. S. Statutes at Large,* XI, 162.

3. For these instructions, see W. Turrentine Jackson, *Wagon Roads West: A Study of Federal Road Surveys and Construction in the Trans-Mississippi West, 1846-1869* (Berkeley, 1952), 221-22.

4. *House Executive Document 108,* 35 Cong., 2 Sess., contains Leach's report of this work.

5. See Jackson, *Wagon Roads West,* 227-32.

6. For details about the life of the teamster, see Oscar O. Winther, *The Transportation Frontier: Trans-Mississippi West, 1865-1890* (New York,

1964), Chapter 3; and Henry P. Walker, *The Wagonmasters: High Plains Freighting from the Earliest Days of the Santa Fe Trail to 1880* (Norman, 1966), Chapter 4.

7. *Rules and Regulations for the Governing of Russell, Majors & Waddell's Outfit* (Nebraska City, 1859), 1-8.

8. Captain Rufus Ingalls to Major General Thomas L. Jessup, Denmark, Maine, September 9, 1853, in Fort Yuma Correspondence, National Archives, RG 94 (microfilm copy). Other estimates of the costs involved in moving goods to Fort Yuma were slightly lower.

9. Jaeger File, Hayden Collection, Arizona Historical Society, Tucson.

10. See Horace Greeley, "The Plains as I Crossed Them Ten Years Ago," *Harper's Monthly*, XXXVIII (May 1869), 790. A good general history of Russell, Majors and Waddell is that of Raymond W. Settle and Mary Lund Settle, *Empire on Wheels* (Stanford, Cal., 1949).

11. Ochoa File, Hayden Collection, Arizona Historical Society, Tucson.

Chapter 6

1. Gertrude Harris, *A Tale of Men Who Knew Not Fear* (San Antonio, 1935), 18. James C. McKee, in his story of this engagement, stated that the Texans had about four hundred men and stated that Baylor's reply to the demand for surrender was, "If he [Lynde] wished the town, to come and take it." See James C. McKee, *Narrative of the Surrender of a Command of U. S. Forces at Fort Fillmore, New Mexico, in July, A.D., 1861* (Houston, 1960; reprint of 1886 original), 18. Lynde declared in his official report that he brought 380 federal troops into battle against 700 Texans; see *The War of the Rebellion: A Compilation of the Official Records of the Union and Confederate Armies* (128 vols.; Washington, D.C., 1880-1901), Series I, IV, 5-6. Hereafter cited as *O.R.*

2. "Report of Mesilla Convention," *O.R.*, IV, 39. For full background details, see B. Sacks, "The Creation of the Territory of Arizona," *Arizona and the West*, V (spring and summer 1963), 112-13. See also the *Mesilla Times* of the appropriate dates.

3. For details about his life, see Max L. Heyman, Jr., *Prudent Soldier: A Biography of Major General E. R. S. Canby, 1817-1873* (Glendale, 1959).

4. For the story of this fight and of its significance, see Walter P. Webb (ed.), *The Handbook of Texas* (2 vols.; Austin, 1952), I, 424.

5. *O.R.*, Series I, I, 577-78.

6. For details, see W. W. Mills, *Forty Years at El Paso* (El Paso, 1962), 50-55.

7. The documents relating to this incredible affair are in *O.R.*, Series I, IV, 1-20. For his actions that day, Lynde was dropped from the rolls of the army

on November 25, 1861, but in 1866 he was restored in rank and placed on the retired list; see *O.R.,* Series I, IV, 15-16. See also Martin H. Hall, "The Skirmish at Mesilla," *Arizona and the West,* I (winter 1959), 343-51; Martin L. Crimmins, "Fort Fillmore," *New Mexico Historical Review,* VI (October 1931), 327-33; and W. A. Keleher, *Turmoil in New Mexico, 1846-1868* (Santa Fe, 1952), 198n.

8. *Mesilla Times,* July 27, 1861, as quoted in Martin H. Hall, "The Mesilla Times: A Journal of Confederate Arizona," *Arizona and the West,* V (winter 1963), 347.

9. The Baylor Proclamation is contained in *O.R.,* Series I, IV, 20-31.

10. *Ibid.,* 22-23.

11. *Journal of the Congress of the Confederate States of America, 1861-1865* (7 vols.; *Senate Document 234,* 58 Cong., 2 Sess.), I, 620, 635, 660-61, 691.

12. *O.R.,* Series IV, I, 853, 858, 930; F. S. Donnell, "The Confederate Territory of Arizona, as Compiled From Official Sources," *New Mexico Historical Review,* XVII (April 1942), 148-63.

13. George W. Baylor, *John Robert Baylor: Confederate Governor of Arizona,* edited by Odie B. Faulk (Tucson, 1966), 33; another version is in Hall, "The Mesilla Times," 349-50.

14. The muster rolls of these two companies are in Martin H. Hall, *Sibley's New Mexico Brigade* (Austin, 1961), 324-26.

15. *O.R.,* Series I, L, Part 1, 942.

16. Theo Noel, *A Campaign from Santa Fe to the Mississippi, Being a History of the Old Sibley Brigade* (Shreveport, La., 1865), 5.

17. W. T. Wroe, "New Mexico Campaign in 1861-62" (manuscript, n.d., Confederate Museum, Austin); Harris, *A Tale of Men Who Knew Not Fear,* 22-25.

18. *O.R.,* Series I, IV, 159.

19. Martin H. Hall, "The Skirmish at Picacho," *Civil War History,* IV (March 1958), 27-36.

20. *O.R.,* Series I, IX, 506-8, 522.

21. *Ibid.,* L, Part 1, 96-97.

22. *Ibid.,* 119-20.

23. *Ibid.,* 98, 120-21.

24. *Ibid.,* 128-33.

25. For details of this campaign, see *O.R.,* Series I, XXVI, Part 1, 255-56.

26. For the defeat of Mangas Coloradas, see Daniel E. Conner, *Joseph Reddiford Walker and the Arizona Adventure* (Norman, 1956).

27. Sacks, "The Creation of the Territory of Arizona," 122-48.

Chapter 7

1. Ochoa File and Tully File, Arizona Historical Society, Tucson. See also Frank C. Lockwood, *Pioneer Portraits: Selected Vignettes* (Tucson, 1968), 71-87.

2. For details about the last days of the Overland on the Southern route, see Conkling and Conkling, *The Butterfield Overland Mail*, II, 325-44.

3. Settle and Settle, *Empire on Wheels,* Chapter 3.

4. For details, see J. V. Frederick, *Ben Holladay: The Stagecoach King* (Glendale, 1940).

5. Samuel Bowles, *Across the Continent: A Summer's Journey* (Springfield, Mass., 1865), 15-16.

6. Noted in J. L. Ringwalt, *Development of Transportation Systems in the United States* (Philadelphia, 1888), 65. See also Neill C. Wilson, *Treasure Express: Epic Days of the Wells Fargo* (New York, 1936), and Edward Hungerford, *Wells Fargo: Advancing the American Frontier* (New York, 1949).

7. Lockwood, *Pioneer Portraits,* 161-77, and Gertrude Hill, "Henry Clay Hooker: King of the Sierra Bonita," *Arizoniana,* II (winter 1961), 12-15.

8. Allen A. Erwin, *The Southwest of John H. Slaughter, 1841-1922* (Glendale, 1965).

9. Most of the details about the telegraph are taken from Norman L. Rue, "Words by Iron Wire: Construction of the Military Telegraph in Arizona Territory, 1873-1877" (MA thesis, University of Arizona, 1967), and from various reports of the secretary of war, as well as the newspapers of the cities along the route.

Chapter 8

1. Joseph Fish Manuscript, Arizona Historical Society, Tucson.

2. "Building the Southern Pacific Railroad Through Arizona," *Arizona Historical Review,* I (January 1929), 103.

3. For involved details about the building of the Southern Pacific, see Stuart Daggett, *Chapters on the History of the Southern Pacific* (New York, 1922), and Neill C. Wilson and Frank J. Taylor, *Southern Pacific: The Roaring Story of a Fighting Railroad* (New York, 1952).

Chapter 9

1. William S. Oury File, Arizona Historical Society, Tucson.

2. Richard Yates, "The Great Cactus Derby of 1914," *Arizona Highways,* XLV (June 1969), 2-9.

Bibliography

Manuscript Sources

John Robert Baylor File, Arizona Historical Society, Tucson.
Philip St. George Cooke File, Arizona Historical Society, Tucson.
George Crook File, Arizona Historical Society, Tucson.
Joseph Fish Manuscript, Arizona Historical Society, Tucson.
John Salmon Ford Memoirs, transcript, 7 vols., Archives, University of Texas Library, Austin.
Fort Yuma Correspondence, National Archives, RG 94 (microfilm copy).
Henry Clay Hooker File, Arizona Historical Society, Tucson.
L. J. F. Jaeger File, Hayden Collection, Arizona Historical Society, Tucson.
Frank Lockwood Collection, Arizona Historical Society, Tucson.
Estevan Ochoa File, Hayden Collection, Arizona Historical Society, Tucson.
Granville Oury File, Hayden Collection, Arizona Historical Society, Tucson.
William S. Oury File, Hayden Collection, Arizona Historical Society, Tucson.
Rue, Norman L., "Words by Iron Wire: Construction of the Military Telegraph in Arizona Territory, 1873-1877," MA thesis, University of Arizona, 1967.
John H. Slaughter File, Arizona Historical Society, Tucson.
P. R. Tully File, Hayden Collection, Arizona Historical Society, Tucson.
W. T. Wroe, "New Mexico Campaign in 1861-62," manuscript, n.d., Confederate Museum, Austin, Texas.

Printed Original Sources

Bailey, L. R. (ed.), *The A. B. Gray Report*. Los Angeles, 1963.
Bartlett, John R. *Personal Narrative of Explorations and Incidents . . .* 2 vols.; New York, 1854, and reprint.
Bean, Lowell J., and William M. Mason. *Diaries and Accounts of the Romero Expeditions in Arizona and California*. Palm Springs, Cal., 1962.
Bell, James G. "A Log of the Texas-California Cattle Trail," edited by J. Evetts Haley. *Southwestern Historical Quarterly,* XXXV and XXXVI (January, April, and July 1932), 208-37, 290-316, 47-66.

Bolton, Herbert E. *Anza's California Expeditions.* 5 vols.; Berkeley, 1930.

Congressional Globe.

Cooke, Philip St. George. *The Conquest of New Mexico and California in 1846-1848.* New York, 1878, and reprint.

———. "Journal of the March of the Mormon Battalion of Infantry Volunteers under the Command of Lieut. Col. P. St. Geo. Cooke . . . ," *Senate Document 2,* 30 Cong., Special Sess.

———. "Report on the March of the Mormon Battalion, February 5, 1847," *House Document 41,* 30 Cong., 1 Sess.

Coues, Elliott (trans. and ed.). *On the Trail of a Spanish Pioneer: The Diary and Itinerary of Francisco Garcés* . . . 2 vols.; New York, 1900.

Couts, Cave J. *From San Diego to the Colorado in 1849: The Journal and Maps of Cave J. Couts,* ed. by William McPherson. Los Angeles, 1932.

Cremony, John C. *Life Among the Apaches.* San Francisco, 1868, and reprint.

Edwards, E. I. (ed.). *The Whipple Report.* Los Angeles, 1961.

Emory, William H. "Report of the United States and Mexican Boundary Commission," *Senate Executive Document 108,* 34 Cong., 1 Sess. 3 vols. in 2.

Faulk, Odie B. (trans. and ed.). *The Constitution of Occidente.* Tucson, 1967.

Hammond, George P. (ed.). *The Treaty of Guadalupe Hidalgo.* Berkeley, 1949.

———, and Edward H. Howes (eds.). *Overland to California on the Southwestern Trail, 1849.* Berkeley, 1950.

Harris, Benjamin B. *The Gila Trail: The Texas Argonauts and the California Gold Rush,* edited by Richard H. Dillon. Norman, 1960.

Hooker, William F. *The Bull-whacker: Adventures of a Frontier Freighter,* edited by Howard R. Driggs. Yonkers, N.Y., 1927.

House Executive Document 108, 35 Cong., 2 Sess.

House Report 81, 33 Cong., 1 Sess.

Journal of the Congress of the Confederate States of America, 1861-1865. 7 vols.; *Senate Document 234,* 58 Cong., 2 Sess.

McKee, James C. *Narrative of the Surrender of a Command of U. S. Forces at Fort Fillmore, New Mexico, in July, A.D. 1861.* Houston, 1960, reprint of 1886 original.

Malloy, William M. (comp.). *Treaties, Conventions, International Acts, Protocols and Agreements Between the United States of America and Other Powers, 1776-1909.* 2 vols.; Washington, D.C., 1910.

Marcy, Randolph B. *Thirty Years of Army Life on the Border.* New York, 1866.

Miller, David H. (ed.). *Treaties and Other International Acts of the United States of America.* 8 vols.; Washington, D.C., 1942-48.

213

Noel, Theo. *A Campaign from Santa Fe to the Mississippi, Being a History of the Old Sibley Brigade.* Shreveport, La., 1865.

Oliphant, J. Orin (ed.). *On the Arkansas Route to California in 1849: The Journal of Robert B. Green of Lewisburg, Pennsylvania.* Lewisburg, Pa., 1955.

Ormsby, Waterman L. *The Butterfield Overland Mail,* edited by Lyle H. Wright and Josephine M. Bynum. San Marino, Cal., 1942.

Pancoast, Charles. *A Quaker Forty-Niner: The Adventures of Charles Edward Pancoast on the American Frontier,* edited by Anna P. Hannum. Philadelphia, 1930.

"Postmaster-General's Report," *Senate Executive Document 3,* 36 Cong., 1 Sess.

"Report of A. B. Gray," *Senate Executive Document 55,* 33 Cong., 2 Sess.

"Report of Captain R. B. Marcy," *Senate Executive Document 64,* 31 Cong., 1 Sess.

"Report of the Committee on Foreign Relations," *Senate Report 345,* 32 Cong., 1 Sess.

"Report of the Secretary of War," *Senate Executive Document 19,* 31 Cong., 2 Sess.

"Reports of Explorations and Surveys," *Senate Executive Document 78,* 33 Cong., 2 Sess., 10 vols.

Rules and Regulations for the Governing of Russell, Majors & Waddell's Outfit. Nebraska City, 1859.

Senate Executive Document 60, 32 Cong., 1 Sess.

Senate Executive Document 119, 32 Cong., 1 Sess.

Strahorn, Carrie A. *Fifteen Thousand Miles by Stage.* New York, 1911.

U. S. Statutes at Large.

The War of the Rebellion: A Compilation of the Official Records of the Union and Confederate Armies. 128 vols.; Washington, D.C., 1880-1901.

Way, Phocion R. "Overland via Jackass Mail in 1858: The Diary of Phocion R. Way," edited by William R. Duffen. *Arizona and the West,* II (1960), 35-53, 147-64, 279-92, 353-70.

Newspapers

Houston *Democratic Telegraph and Register.*

Mesilla Times.

New York *Herald.*

Prescott *Arizona Miner.*

San Diego *Daily Union.*

San Francisco *Daily Alta California.*

Tucson *Arizona Daily Citizen.*

Secondary Sources: Books

Albright, George L. *Official Explorations for Pacific Railroads, 1853-1855,* edited by H. E. Bolton. Berkeley, 1921.

Baldwin, Gordon. *The Warrior Apaches.* Tucson, 1966.

Banning, William, and George H. *Six Horses.* New York, 1930.

Barnes, Will C. *Apaches and Longhorns.* Los Angeles, 1941.

Baylor, George W. *John Robert Baylor: Confederate Governor of Arizona,* edited by Odie B. Faulk, Tucson, 1966.

Bieber, Ralph P., and Averam B. Bender (eds.). *Exploring Southwestern Trails* (vol. 7 in *The Southwest Historical Series*). Glendale, Cal., 1938.

Bieber, Ralph P., and LeRoy R. Hafen (eds.). *The Southwest Historical Series.* 12 vols.; Glendale, Cal., 1931-43.

Bowles, Samuel. *Across the Continent: A Summer's Journey.* Springfield, Mass., 1865.

Brandes, Ray. *Frontier Military Posts of Arizona.* Globe, Ariz., 1960.

Callcott, Wilfrid H. *Santa Anna: The Story of an Enigma Who Once Was Mexico.* Norman, 1936.

Chapman, Arthur. *The Pony Express.* New York, 1932.

Clarke, D. L. *Stephen Watts Kearny: Soldier of the West.* Norman, 1961.

Conkling, Roscoe P. and Margaret B. *The Butterfield Overland Mail, 1857-1869.* 2 vols.; Glendale, Cal., 1947.

Conner, Daniel E. *Joseph Reddiford Walker and the Arizona Adventure.* Norman, 1956.

Connor, Seymour V., and Odie B. Faulk. *North America Divided: The Mexican War, 1846-1848.* New York, 1971.

Daggett, Stuart. *Chapters on the History of the Southern Pacific.* New York, 1922.

Dickson, Arthur J. *Covered Wagon Days.* Cleveland, 1929.

Dillon, Richard H. *Fool's Gold: The Decline and Fall of Captain John Sutter of California.* New York, 1967.

Duval, John C. *The Adventures of Big-Foot Wallace.* Lincoln, 1935, and reprint.

Egan, Ferol. *The El Dorado Trail: The Story of the Gold Rush Routes Across Mexico.* New York, 1970.

Erwin, Allan A. *The Southwest of John H. Slaughter, 1841-1922.* Glendale, Cal., 1965.

Farish, Thomas E. *The History of Arizona.* 8 vols.; Phoenix, 1915.

Ferris, Robert G. (ed.). *Prospector, Cowhand, and Sodbuster: Historic Places Associated with the Mining, Ranching, and Farming Frontiers in the Trans-Mississippi West.* Washington, D.C., 1967.

Foreman, Grant (ed.). *Marcy and the Gold Seekers*. Norman, 1937.

Frederick, J. V. *Ben Holladay: The Stagecoach King*. Glendale, Cal., 1940.

Galloway, John D. *The First Transcontinental Railroad*. New York, 1950.

Garber, Paul N. *The Gadsden Treaty*. Gloucester, Mass., 1959.

Golder, Frank A., Thomas A. Bailey, and J. Lyman Smith. *The March of the Mormon Battalion*. New York, 1928.

Goodwin, Grenville. *The Social Organization of the Western Apaches*. New York, 1938.

Hafen, LeRoy R. *The Overland Mail, 1849-1869*. Cleveland, 1926.

Hall, Martin H. *Sibley's New Mexico Brigade*. Austin, 1961.

Harris, Gertrude. *A Tale of Men Who Knew Not Fear*. San Antonio, 1935.

Heyman, Max L., Jr. *Prudent Soldier: A Biography of Major General E. R. S. Canby, 1817-1873*. Glendale, Cal., 1959.

Hine, Robert V. *Bartlett's West: Drawing the Mexican Boundary*. New Haven, 1968.

Hollon, Eugene. *Beyond the Cross Timbers: The Travels of Randolph B. Marcy, 1812-1887*. Norman, 1955.

Horn, Calvin. *New Mexico's Troubled Years*. Albuquerque, 1963.

Hungerford, Edward. *Wells Fargo: Advancing the American Frontier*. New York, 1949.

Jackson, W. Turrentine. *Wagon Roads West: A Study of Federal Road Surveys and Construction in the Trans-Mississippi West, 1846-1869*. Berkeley, 1952.

Keleher, W. A. *Turmoil in New Mexico, 1846-1868*. Santa Fe, 1952.

Lang, Walter B. *The First Overland Mail: Butterfield Trail*. East Aurora, N.Y., 1940.

Lewis, Oscar. *The Big Four*. New York, 1938.

Lockwood, Frank C. *Pioneer Portraits: Selected Vignettes*. Tucson, 1968.

Mills, W. W. *Forty Years at El Paso*. El Paso, 1962.

Ochoa, Humberto Escoto. *Integración y Desintegración de Nuestra Frontera Norte*. Mexico City, 1949.

Opler, Morris E. *An Apache Life-Way*. Chicago, 1941.

Raht, Carlysle G. *The Romance of Davis Mountains and Big Bend Country*. Odessa, Tex., 1963.

Reed, S. G. *A History of the Texas Railroads*. Houston, 1941.

Ringwalt, J. L. *Development of Transportation Systems in the United States*. Philadelphia, 1888.

Rippy, J. Fred. *The United States and Mexico*. New York, 1931.

Roberts, Brigham H. *The Mormon Battalion: Its History and Achievements*. Salt Lake City, 1919.

Russel, Robert T. *Improvement of Communication with the Pacific Coast as an Issue in American Politics, 1783-1864*. Cedar Rapids, Iowa, 1948.

Settle, Raymond W., and Mary Lund. *Empire on Wheels*. Stanford, 1949.

216

Spicer, Edward H. *Cycles of Conquest.* Tucson, 1962.

Stinson, A. L. *History of the Express Business.* New York, 1881.

Stratton, R. B. *Captivity of the Oatman Girls.* New York, 1859, and reprint.

Tallack, William. *The California Overland Express.* Los Angeles, 1935.

Thompson, Robert L. *Wiring a Continent: The History of the Telegraph Industry in the United States, 1832-1866.* Princeton, 1947.

Twitchell, Ralph E. *The Leading Facts of New Mexican History.* 2 vols.; Cedar Rapids, Iowa, 1911-12.

Tyler, Daniel. *Concise History of the Mormon Battalion in the Mexican War.* Salt Lake City, 1881, and reprint.

Walker, Henry P. *The Wagonmasters: High Plains Freighting from the Earliest Days of the Santa Fe Trail to 1880.* Norman, 1966.

Webb, Walter P. (ed.). *The Handbook of Texas.* 2 vols.; Austin, 1952.

Wilson, Neill C. *Southern Pacific: The Roaring Story of a Fighting Railroad.* New York, 1952.

————. *Treasure Express: Epic Days of the Wells Fargo.* New York, 1936.

Winther, Oscar O. *Express and Stagecoach Days.* Stanford, 1936.

————. *The Transportation Frontier: Trans-Mississippi West, 1865-1890.* New York, 1964.

————. *Via Western Express and Stagecoach.* Stanford, 1945.

Young, Otis E., Jr. *The West of Philip St. George Cooke, 1809-1895.* Glendale, Cal., 1955.

Zollinger, James P. *Sutter: The Man and His Empire.* New York, 1939.

Zorrilla, Luis G. *Historia de las Relaciones entre Mexico y Los Estados Unidos de America, 1800-1958.* 2 vols.; Mexico City, 1965-66.

Secondary Sources: Articles

Almada, Francisco R. "Governadores del Estado: Gral. D. Ángel Trias," *Boletín de la Sociedad Chihuahuense de Esudios Historicos,* III (July and August 1941), 172-88.

Bailey, W. F. "Overland by Butterfield Stage," *Sunset,* March 1907.

Beattie, George W. "Diary of a Ferryman and Trader at Fort Yuma," *Society of California Pioneers Quarterly,* XIV (1929).

Bigler, Henry W. "Extracts from the Journal of Henry W. Bigler," *Utah Historical Quarterly,* V (April 1932), 35-64.

Brinckerhoff, Sidney B. "Passport to Mexico," *The Journal of Arizona History,* VIII (spring 1967), 54-59.

"Building the Southern Pacific Railroad Through Arizona," *Arizona Historical Review,* I (January 1929), 97-104.

Crimmins, Martin L. "Fort Fillmore," *New Mexico Historical Review,* VI (October 1931), 327-33.

Cross, Jack L. "The El Paso-Fort Yuma Wagon Road, 1857-1860," *Password*, IV (Nos. 1 and 2, 1959), 4-18, 58-70.

Donnell, F. S. "The Confederate Territory of Arizona, as Compiled From Official Sources," *New Mexico Historical Review*, XVII (April 1942), 148-63.

Ewing, Floyd F., Jr. "The Mule as a Factor in the Development of the Southwest," *Arizona and the West*, V (winter 1963), 315-26.

Faulk, Odie B., and Sidney B. Brinckerhoff. "Soldiering at the End of the World," *The American West*, III (summer 1966), 28-37.

Greeley, Horace. "The Plains as I Crossed Them Ten Years Ago," *Harper's Monthly*, XXXVIII (May 1869), 790.

Greenwood, C. L. (ed.). "Opening Routes to El Paso, 1849," *Southwestern Historical Quarterly*, XLVIII (October 1944), 262-74.

Greever, William S. "Railway Development in the Southwest," *New Mexico Historical Review*, XXXII (April 1957), 151-203.

Hall, Martin H. "The Mesilla Times: A Journal of Confederate Arizona," *Arizona and the West*, V (winter 1963), 337-51.

———. "The Skirmish at Mesilla," *Arizona and the West*, I (winter 1959), 343-51.

———. "The Skirmish at Picacho," *Civil War History*, IV (March 1958), 27-36.

Hargrave, Maria. "Overland by Ox Train in 1870," Historical Society of Southern California *Quarterly*, XXVI (January 1944), 9-37.

Hill, Gertrude. "Henry Clay Hooker: King of the Sierra Bonita," *Arizoniana*, II (winter 1961), 12-15.

Hinton, H. P., Jr. "John Simpson Chisum, 1877-1884," *New Mexico Historical Review*, XXXI (July 1956), 177-205, and XXXII (January 1957), 53-65.

Hollon, W. Eugene. "Great Days of the Overland Stage," *American Heritage*, VIII (June 1957), 27-31, 101.

Jones, Nathaniel V. "Journal of Nathaniel V. Jones, with the Mormon Battalion," *Utah Historical Quarterly*, IV (January 1931), 6-24.

Lesley, Lewis B. "A Southern Transcontinental Railroad into California: Texas & Pacific vs. Southern Pacific, 1865-1885," *Pacific Historical Review*, V (January 1936), 52-60.

Lummis, Charles F. "Pioneer Transportation in Arizona," *McClure's Magazine*, October, 1905.

McClintock, William A. "Journal of a Trip through Texas and Northern Mexico in 1846-1847," *Southwestern Historical Quarterly*, XXXIV (January 1931), 231-56.

Mahon, Emmie Giddings W., and Chester V. Kielman. "George H. Giddings and the San Antonio-San Diego Mail Line," *Southwestern Historical Quarterly*, LXI (October 1957), 220-59.

Martin, Mabelle E. "California Emigrant Roads Through Texas," *Southwestern Historical Quarterly*, XXVIII (April 1925), 287-301.

Matthews, William R. "An Answer to a Century-Old Question," Tucson *Arizona Daily Star*, September 15, 1965.

Neighbours, Kenneth F. (ed.). "The Report of the Expedition of Major Robert S. Neighbors to El Paso in 1849," *Southwestern Historical Quarterly*, LX (April 1957), 527-32.

Sacks, B. "The Creation of the Territory of Arizona," *Arizona and the West*, V (spring and summer 1963), 29-62, 104-48.

———. "New Evidence on the Bascom Affair," *Arizona and the West*, IV (autumn 1962), 261-78.

Smith, Ralph A. "Apache 'Ranching' Below the Gila, 1841-1845," *Arizoniana*, III (winter 1962), 1-17.

———. "The Scalp Hunter in the Borderlands," *Arizona and the West*, VI (spring 1964), 5-22.

Thonhoff, Robert H. "San Antonio Stage Lines, 1847-1881, *Southwestern Studies*, No. 29 (1971).

Utley, Robert M. "The Bascom Affair: A Reconstruction," *Arizona and the West*, III (spring 1961), 59-68.

Yates, Richard. "The Great Cactus Derby of 1914," *Arizona Highways*, XLV (June 1969), 2-9.

Index

226

227

229